FROM DALÍ TO AI

DESIGN

REALISM

&

the
DESIGN
MUSEUM

NOW

CONTENTS

Surrealism was launched in 1924 in the spirit of revolution against the tyranny of rationalism. It was embraced first by poets and philosophers 'out of the ashes of Dada', in the words of its self-proclaimed leader André Breton, and then by artists. It's fair to say that design was relatively late to the Surrealist movement, but from the mid 1930s the aesthetic impact of what Breton described as 'convulsive beauty' began to appear in fashion and furniture design, and it remains an enduring influence for many designers working today.

This trajectory is explored to the present day in the exhibition *Objects of Desire: Surrealism and Design 1924 –Today*. The project was produced by the Vitra Design Museum and it has already travelled extensively – a testament to Surrealism's global impact as well as to the quality of curatorial vision. In an extension of the original exhibition and in the spirit of collaboration, we have added a series of new contemporary pieces here at the Design Museum in London, from groundbreaking couture by Daniel Roseberry for Maison Schiaparelli, Mary Katrantzou, Maison Margiela and Cinzia Ruggeri, to British artists and designers including Sarah Lucas, Jonathan Trayte, Vince Fraser and Dunne & Raby. This book, *Surrealism and Design Now: From Dali to AI*, explores the contemporary resonance of Surrealism in a whole range of fields of design, from interiors and fashion to craft and furniture. It also examines the impact of a cultural movement that is a century old on the future-facing disciplines of speculative design and AI.

The staging of *Objects of Desire* at the Design Museum relied on the generous advice and expertise of many external partners. The Tate have been exceptionally helpful with loans and I'd like to thank Maria Balshaw and her staff for being so collegial. Above all, though, I'd like to thank Mateo Kries, director of the Vitra Design Museum and curator for the *Objects of Desire* exhibition. Both the idea and the realisation of the exhibition are down to him and it has been a pleasure to collaborate with the Vitra team in developing the exhibition for London. ▪▪▪▪

TIM MARLOW
Chief Executive and Director of the Design Museum

KATHRYN JOHNSON

ABSOLUTE REALITY

Surrealism recognises dreams and desires as our constant companions. The 1924 *Manifesto of Surrealism* by poet André Breton called for a fusion between the day-lit world of conscious thought and the murkier realms of dreams and the subconscious:

> I believe in the future resolution of these two
> states, dream and reality, which are seemingly
> so contradictory, into a kind of absolute reality,
> a *surreality*, if one may so speak.[1]

1. André Breton, 'First Surrealist Manifesto' (1924), in *Manifestoes of Surrealism, trans.* Richard Seaver and Helen R. Lane (Ann Arbor: University of Michigan Press, 1969), 14.

Since then, the emphasis on the fantastical and absurd in Surrealist art has often led to the perception that the movement was divorced from the reality of everyday life. Paying attention to Surrealism's engagement with the designed world helps to correct the balance. It is arguably through design that Breton and other early Surrealists came closest to achieving one of their central aims: to change our understanding of what reality is and how it is experienced.

Today, breakthroughs in the design of artificial intelligence (AI) in tandem with advances in neuroscience are also causing us to revise our notions of reality. It is increasingly clear that Breton was on the right track, although operating with a skewed model of consciousness derived from his reading of Freudian psychoanalysis. The fusion between dream and reality he had called for had already taken place. We are beginning to appreciate that the unconscious plays a crucial role in our thought processes at all hours of the day, and human intelligence cannot be equated with rationality as once supposed. 'Absolute reality or *surreality*' may be, simply, reality.

It is instructive that those who attempted to create artificial intelligences based on logical, goal-orientated frameworks in the twentieth century failed to reach their goal. It was only in the 2010s that machine learning began to produce convincing results, when computer programs were modelled on the architecture of the brain as 'neural networks' and set to iterate freely in an unpredictable way. A truly awe-inspiring conjunction of computer science, design and engineering expertise led to this breakthrough, but the most impressive achievement was the decision to relinquish control.

Such insights confirm that the Surrealists were right to pay attention to the unconscious, to champion free association and elevate the marvellous and impossible. These are the pathways to effective learning and communication – whether in humans or machines – and creative breakthroughs across all disciplines, including design. A shared interest in the creative power of unconscious thought and irrational, imaginative leaps comes through in interviews with leading contemporary designers in these pages.

Dunne & Raby, pioneers of speculative design, speak of making 'forays into the unreal' and designing 'impossible objects'. Their work reveals the limits we place on the design imagination, and challenges us to expand our notions of what twenty-first-century reality is and can be. The founder of Google's Artists + Machine Intelligence programme, Blaise Agüera y Arcas, characterises the operation of human intelligence and AI as an excitingly messy and unpredictable sequence of reactions and 'remixes'. Humberto Campana, one half of the Brazilian design powerhouse Estudio Campana, brings a similar understanding to the world of product design when he reflects, 'People think things need to be very rational, when there is a better way to construct things, through contamination.'[2]

2 Humberto Campana in 'The Campana Brothers', *Surrealism and Design Now: From Dalí to AI*, ed. Kathryn Johnson (London: Design Museum, 2022), 58.

One way to understand the Campana brothers' principle of 'contamination' is by looking at their first chair made from stuffed toys – Banquette (2002). This unique hybrid object made from mass-produced stuffed toys yokes together wildly different ideas and textures. Each element 'contaminates' the other in joyous defiance of restraint and refined tastes.

There is a fascinating parallel between a design like the Campanas' and the lines by the nineteenth-century French poet Lautréamont that the founding Surrealists turned to in the 1920s, 'Beautiful as the chance meeting on a dissecting table of a sewing machine and an umbrella.'[3]

3 Comte de Lautréamont, *Maldoror and Poems* (New York: Penguin, 1978), 216-17.

Lautréamont was describing a sixteen-year-old youth, but the early Surrealists adopted the metaphor as an ideal of beauty. They began in the 1920s to make curious hybrids from everyday objects: an iron studded with nails; a chair with both arms *and* hands. The transition from designing such objects to shaping the designed world was rapid. By the mid-1930s, Surrealism's energising and disruptive impact was felt across architecture and interior design, furniture, fashion and film. The resulting aesthetics were founded on the same principles of unexpected juxtaposition, connection and hybridisation – or, in a single word, contamination. Alyce Mahon deftly explains Surrealism's liberating, object-orientated aesthetics and traces a line from the famous Surrealist objects created by Meret Oppenheim or Dorothea Tanning, to the contemporary work of artists and designers including Sarah Lucas and Najla El Zein.

There have always been those inside and outside the Surrealist movement who perceive design as a trivialisation of Surrealism's higher artistic purpose. Mateo Kries, director of the Vitra Design Museum and curator of the exhibition *Objects of Desire: Surrealism and Design 1924 – Today*, counters this response in his conversation with Tim Marlow, director of the Design Museum. As Kries observes, Surrealism successfully challenged the separation of art and design. Many of the best-known expressions of Surrealism in visual culture were the result of creative practitioners who worked fluidly across the boundaries of both disciplines.

Dali, for one, drew no distinction between his art practice and the design of Surrealist objects such as the Mae West Lips sofa and Lobster Telephones. Both these iconic designs were commissioned and realised by Dali's patron and collector, the wealthy poet Edward James, for his own home. Home interiors, with their clear psychological and emotional aspects, provided the context for some of the first designs informed by Surrealist aesthetics. As Ghislaine Wood observes in her discussion of contemporary designers Gitta Gschwendtner and Nina Saunders, the home continues to be one of the key areas for Surrealist-inspired design today.

4 Sidney Shallett, 'It's the Craziest Business!', *Saturday Evening Post* (14 June 1952). Quoted in Dilys Blum, *Shocking! The Art and Fashion of Elsa Schiaparelli* (Philadelphia: Philadelphia Museum of Art, 2003), 254.

Dali described his design work, alongside his equally successful work with fashion designer Elsa Schiaparelli, as 'propaganda for the imagination', stating, 'The modern artist should participate in every kind of extracurricular activity. Michelangelo designed the dress for the Pope's Swiss Guards. It is all part of the propaganda of your imagination, no?' [4]

Susanna Brown quotes this phrase in her chapter on Surrealism's continued influence on fashion photography and the work of photographer Tim Walker. In collaboration with the actress Tilda Swinton, Walker staged a spectacular fashion shoot in Edward James' extravagant architectural folly 'Las Pozas' (The Pools) in Mexico. Surrealism and fashion have proven to be natural partners since the 1930s, allowing for a joint exploration of the body as both a canvas and a site for performative self-expression.

It is clear that Surrealism's legacy for contemporary design is more than an aesthetic. It is also an attitude. Surrealism helps to liberate design from the rational and utilitarian. It challenges the modern design principle of 'form follows function', because it is alive to the emotional and psychological impact of even the most ordinary objects. It perceives that imagination is not an 'add-on', but a crucial facet of human experience. To borrow the words of Japanese designer Shiro Kuramata, 'Enchantment can also be considered a function'.

Over the last hundred years, design has evolved in dialogue with these ideas. There are direct lines of influence, of course. Daniel Roseberry at Maison Schiaparelli continues to work in the groundbreaking spirit of the house's legendary founder, Elsa Schiaparelli. Jasper Morrison channels the Duchampian ready-made with his Handlebar Table (1982) – as Gae Aulenti also does with the table Tour (1993), which glides across the room on bicycle wheels. Yet Surrealism's impact on contemporary design is often less obvious, and all the more intriguing for it, as Glenn Adamson demonstrates in his fascinating discussion of the unexpected relevance of Surrealism to post-1950s craft practice.

At certain moments, the conceptually driven design that Surrealism helped to initiate has moved to the forefront of innovation. One such moment came in the 1960s and 1970s with the exuberant rise of Radical Design and the wildly imaginative architectural concepts of studios such as Archigram. Taking key inspiration from that era, designers Dunne & Raby ushered in another period of original and conceptually driven design following the financial crash of 2008. The rise of Afro-Surrealism as a distinct, powerful and popular movement in art and design can also be charted from the 2010s.

It is no accident that these moments coincide with periods of geopolitical conflict, economic instability and fear of the future. Surrealism was in part a reaction to the horrors of the First World War (1914-18) and the 1918 influenza pandemic. Its tenets were founded on a creative embrace of chaos. Focused on universal aspects of human experience, Surrealism inspired designers not only to change the material world but to expand our inner worlds too: our attitudes, thoughts and imagination.

Today, in the context of dizzying technological change, war and the Covid-19 global pandemic, the Surrealist spirit feels urgent and relevant once again. The torch has now been passed to contemporary artists and designers, and to all those who dare to shake up the creative process, discover new tools and think differently. ▪▪▪▪▪▪

Tim Marlow, chief executive and director of the
Design Museum, spoke to Mateo Kries, director of the
Vitra Design Museum. Marlow is a writer, broadcaster
and art historian, and was previously artistic director
of the Royal Academy of Arts and director of exhibitions
at White Cube. Kries joined the Vitra Design Museum
as a curator in 1995, and has brought his expertise in
design to a programme of groundbreaking exhibitions
since taking the helm as director in 2011. He curated
the 2019 exhibition *Objects of Desire: Surrealism
and Design 1924 – Today*.

TM When I first heard about the *Objects of
Desire* exhibition, I imagined you'd looked
at Surrealism and its history, and then
explored its influence up to the present day.
Then I wondered whether you'd actually
been looking at contemporary design, and
retraced its roots back to Surrealism. So was
it the past that informed your involvement
with the present? Or was it the present that
triggered your interest in the past?

MATE▬O KRIE▬S

MK It was really both. As an art historian, I'm
not only interested in design but also in the
evolution of modern art within the context of
design. That said, it was more from a design
perspective — not only contemporary design
but also post-war design of the 1960s and 70s.
  Walking through the halls of our
collection, I'd often see design pieces which
I knew we weren't likely to exhibit: somehow
they didn't quite fit into any category. And
then one day, I thought that Surrealism would
provide the right context in which to explore
them. So it really came down to looking at

TIM MA▬LOW
our own collection.

TM All of which implies that Surrealism is outside the mainstream of classic Modernist discourse. At the same time, it's interesting to see where Surrealism influences the mainstream. Le Corbusier, for example, had an on-off relationship with Surrealism, which transcends that kind of clichéd view of him being all about machine aesthetics.

MK Yes, absolutely. What we wanted to do was to connect two discourses. The Surrealist discourse had been connected to the daily object through Marcel Duchamp and the ready-mades, and through the Surrealist objects of Salvador Dalí, André Breton and others. But it had not been connected to any broader discourse on design and architecture. This only happened in very specialised academic texts.

You mentioned Le Corbusier. I always thought that he was more than a rationalist. Besides being interested in industry and reduced forms, he was also interested in visual effects and narrative spaces. It's quite a different interpretation of Le Corbusier, and one which links him very much to Surrealism. From then on, you can retrace an alternative narrative of architecture and design in Modernist times. Alvar Aalto, for example, was interested in the emotional and sensual aspects of architecture, and of course, in organic forms — all aspects central to Surrealism.

Vitra Design Museum, 2019. Installation view of *Objects of Desire: Surrealism and Design 1924 – Today* exhibition

TM Surrealism at its heart is playful and takes on board the idea of the absurd and the role of humour. Yet, even from within the movement, there's a feeling that its expansion into design somehow trivialises Surrealism. You are reclaiming that territory to a certain extent, aren't you?

Vitra Design Museum, 2019. Installation view
of *Objects of Desire: Surrealism and Design
1924 - Today* exhibition

MK Yes, and of course we are used to the art world looking at design as a kind of trivialisation. I'm not afraid of that, because as someone working at a design museum, you're constantly confronted with that misunderstanding.

Salvador Dali, for example, was happy to use this as a provocation. He even designed advertising for stockings, and he was happy that the art world was upset about this. I'd say that the trivialisation — which I would rather call 'popularisation' — is a way to create a tension, and to ask a question about the relationship between art and design.

But at that time, there was this critique that the moment a certain art movement reached the world of design and popular culture, it was dead — because it became linked to the spheres of function and economy. However, the Surrealists themselves

Surrealism is not a prescriptive art movement that

had claimed that they wanted to reach people and change things in their lives, so I think this shows the paradox within the success of Surrealism. Looking at Surrealism from a design perspective, we were interested in its transgression into the design world. It happened within the time of Surrealism, in the 1930s and 40s, but it went on into the 60s and 70s and beyond. That's what we're interested in: telling the story of the Surrealist attitude that continues to this day.

TM It's interesting how you used the word transgression just now, and actually design in some ways is a transgression of a purist view of Surrealism.

MK I think it's transgressive in that it rejects the definition of design as merely an industrial practice, as a service by a

designer for a manufacturer. It's looking
at design as something that can involve
speculation, and even contradiction. It uses
strategies similar to the Surrealist artist;
it's transgressing the established definition
of what design is meant to be. This is
an understanding of design that has
been very present in the last two decades.
It was not the common understanding
of design in the post-war years.

TM But design is as much about ideas
as it is about things or objects, and the
power of objects to trigger certain ideas
is essential, isn't it?

MK Yes, absolutely. Objects are triggers
for memories, for unexpected encounters,
and that brings us to the famous definition
of Surrealism.

TM 'The chance encounter of an umbrella and
a sewing machine on a dissecting table.'

tells you how to think, or how you must be. **TM**

MK Exactly. I think that you couldn't
give a better explanation of why design
is relevant in the context of Surrealism,
because we are constantly seeing chance
encounters of objects. I've been speaking
to many designers about how new ideas
come about, including Konstantin Grcic.
He's been collecting objects in his studio
that seem to have nothing in common, but
suddenly they start a dialogue. It's nothing
he can plan, and it's the unplanned that
often brings up a new idea. Similarly, Ronan
Bouroullec's drawings have a meditative
character and are very close to what the
Surrealists were calling *écriture automatique*
or *dessin automatique* — automatic drawing.
Automatic in this sense doesn't mean
machine-like: it means you lose control.

TM You lose control and it's the subject manifesting itself.

MK Exactly. You let your hand draw, and then you look at it afterwards. You can discover things that you wouldn't have discovered when taking a rational and linear approach.

TM And Surrealism is a kind of revolutionary attack on the rational, isn't it?

Yes, it's more an invitation to liberate yourself

MK When Surrealism emerged, the predominant art movements were about the rational world. They were fascinated with machine culture, and with the reflection of a new industrial age. While the Surrealists were a counter-reaction to this, they weren't rejecting industrialisation or the modern era: they were subverting it. And that's what designers often do. Of course, they're not naïve. They're not thinking, like certain movements in the nineteenth century, that we should go back to the Middle Ages, but that instead we should use industrial technologies differently.

There's another interesting appearance of Surrealism in the contemporary design world, where designers use new or digital technologies, like 3D printing, as a process that involves chance and surprise. Two examples from the exhibition are the Sketch Chair by Front Design, and the vases by Audrey Large, which look like random and chaotic forms but are realised with very new technologies. For me, this comes close to the idea of hacking technologies and using them differently.

TM At the moment, there's a strong interest culturally, and within the museum world, in Surrealism. There have been various monographic shows, including those looking at women Surrealists who have previously been overlooked. The Met and then the Tate have been looking at Surrealism as an international movement. The 2022 Venice Biennale was absolutely centred on the idea of dreams and Surrealism. Why do you think it's chiming so much now?

MK Well, I think it's because we are living in a time where the canon — the classical canon, or you could say the Western, male, rational understanding of art and design — is being questioned. Surrealism has a lot of elements that are part of this counter-movement, whether it's the important role of women in Surrealism, which has long been overlooked, or the importance of the mythical and of non-linear thinking.

We are living in a time that's hard to explain, or understand. Surrealism doesn't aim to understand everything, or to explain everything. It accepts the inexplicable.

In fact, it was the same in the 1920s and 1930s when Surrealism came about. That was also a time of major tensions and conflicts in society; a lot of known or established values were shifting. I think we are living in a similar time. We are living in surreal times.

TM I agree. Surrealism has that capacity to engage with the individual experience and imagination, but not in the sense of obsessive individualism. Surrealism is not a prescriptive art movement that tells you how to think, or how you must be. It's not dominated by one style. Taste is quite an expansive idea in Surrealism. It allows for a kind of pluralism, without being completely nebulous.

from any kind of limitations or burdens, to discover what can happen when

MK Yes, it's more an invitation to liberate yourself from any kind of limitations or burdens, to discover what can happen when you follow that liberation. I think that's an attitude that a lot of people feel very close to today. It has something anarchic. It's probably also the art movement in modern history which is most open, and least linked to Western culture.

It's also about how you tell history. There's this idea that modern history has to be rewritten and retold in a different way. I think revisiting how modern history has been written is probably very close to the Surrealist idea of rewriting everything. Breton even made a dictionary of Surrealist things. It's megalomaniacal, of course. He wanted not only to create Surrealist artwork and literature, but also to give new meanings to the words we use. It's a kind of linguistic or encyclopaedic approach, and that is another aspect which feels very close to many approaches in art and design today. Everything is being questioned. I think that, where other art forms at the time were much more about limiting themselves or restricting themselves, Surrealism was all about abundance and thinking big.

TM Do you think that we have reached the end of the main thrust of Surrealism's influence in design with critical and speculative design? Or do you think it will be a fertile, ongoing sequence of narratives?

you follow that liberation. **MK**

MK The tension between the two poles in design — the industrial, rational pole on one side, and the emotional, subjective pole on the other — will always be the tension that defines design. Many designers have to cope with both poles and see how they can exist between them.

So I don't think the influence of Surrealism is a phenomenon that will disappear. Maybe there will be a counter-movement in the next decade, but I think future generations of designers will rediscover Surrealism as an inspiration.

I'd say the era of speculative design and critical design is not yet over, but it's currently shifting towards more political and activist approaches.

At the same time, we've been seeing over the last five to ten years an interesting aesthetic which, although not yet underpinned by theoretical thinking, gets very close to Surrealism. Designers like Audrey Large or Odd Matter or Jonathan Trayte — their aesthetics recall a kind of Neo-Brutalism, a Neo-Primitivism, often using plastic in a very sculptural way. I believe they speak to Surrealism too.

Or, think of those big, thick sneakers which are currently en vogue. Maybe they can't be contextualised within Surrealism's influence, but I'd say they represent a liberation from functionalism. Dali spoke of 'obsessive objects' — I think that gets quite close to what some contemporary design objects are, and I'm saying this in a positive sense. Obsessions are human, and design has to recognise this.

Vitra Design Museum, 2019. Installation view of *Objects of Desire: Surrealism and Design 1924 - Today* exhibition

TM Well, let's pick this theme up in twenty years' time, Mateo, and make it into another exhibition. ▬▬

INTERIO

Nina Saunders, *The Whirlwind is in the Thorn Bush* (detail), 2017

R

DESIGN

DISRUPTIVE INTERIORS

The depiction of the domestic interior and, particularly, the home is a psychologically rich theme in Surrealism. The home was an idea deeply embedded in Freudian and, by extension, Surrealist thought, and provided a topology of symbolic spaces. Its structures, from door and window to attic and stair, have, from Freud on, become constituents of dream analysis and litter the imagery of Surrealism, mapping the emotive on to physical structures in ways that fundamentally shift notions of the home. Through Freudian dream analysis, the home no longer signified security but carried a range of more disturbing and sexualised meanings that fuelled the Surrealists' interests. But the home could represent a myriad of psychological concerns, not least because it was one of the prescribed areas for Modernist interrogation. The desire to counter a technologically driven, rationalist vision of the home undoubtedly contributes to its prominence within Surrealist production, and it continues to shape approaches to design and the interior today.

One of the earliest and most influential Surrealist texts on the home was written by the French poet Louis Aragon. His 'Projet de réforme des habitations' ('Project to reform habitations'), published in the magazine *Littérature* in 1920 under a pseudonym, established a series of poetic concepts for the home that included anthropomorphism, the elision of the organic and inorganic, and the human and animal. Taking the form of a list, a device suggestive of the Surrealist technique of automatic association, it describes the areas of a house and its furnishings. For furniture, Aragon lists:

> *6. Living chairs, hangings of caresses, beds of captive birds. – 7. Different kinds of chairs, their decoration bloody. – 8. Chairs with animal feet.*[1]

1 Germain Dubourg, 'Projet de réforme des habitations: Part II', *Littérature*, 17 (December 1920), 9.

The text markedly rejects the rationalist language of Modernism, establishing an elision of the psychological and the physical that was to become a feature of later Surrealist writing and practice. Aragon describes 'emotional decoration', 'living chairs' and 'beds of captive birds', and – in the specification for 'bedrooms to die in', 'bedrooms to be born in' and 'bedrooms to desire' – he asserted the sociological and emotive function of a room. For him, the interior must have the capacity to convey the historical trace of previous events, contents and inhabitants, the silhouettes of long-gone furniture leaving their marks on the wall of a room. Aragon continued to explore the psychological implications of the interior in later works, and these ideas were tremendously influential for how interior design would assimilate Surrealist ideas. Surrealism continues to provide an alternative to prevailing views of modern design and traditional concepts of the home.

Leonora Carrington's *The Old Maids*, painted after the Second World War in 1947 in Mexico, disrupts notions of the bourgeois interior and traditional representations of domesticity. It is a strange, delicate and powerful image, in which a group of female figures and animals occupy a kitchen space, gently sharing tea. At the centre of the painting, a magical child wears a white halo and black shroud, while a monkey, magpies, a yellow bird and a cat are protagonists whose symbolism is mysterious. The key to understanding the

Leonora Carrington, *The Old Maids*, 1947

scene appears to lie beyond our grasp. *The Old Maids* elides Carrington's preoccupation with folklore, religion, animal symbolism and the occult in the lives of women, but also speaks to the wider theme of Surrealism's disruption of structures of power and patriarchy, particularly in the realm of the domestic. Indeed, many women Surrealists, including Leonor Fini, Meret Oppenheim, Remedios Varo and Carrington, chose to focus on the domestic as a way of challenging norms and establishing new imaginative spheres marked by the feminine. The legacy of Surrealism's reconfiguring of the interior can be seen in the work of many practitioners today, who continue to use the domestic to disrupt ideas of utility and traditional economic and social structures.

Contemporary designer Nina Saunders uses the canvas of the domestic to explore ideas about what is functional, creating witty and often subversive works. Known for her distorting upholstery and reworking of second-hand and found objects, she invests pieces with a range of psychological concerns that recall Aragon's poetic reconfiguring of the domestic and, in particular, his call for 'living chairs'. Her sofa titled *The Age of Reason* (1995) renders a red leather chesterfield redundant as a functional piece of furniture by the insertion of a giant ball under its immaculate buttoned-leather skin. A string of associations are triggered by this incongruously inserted form, which range across impregnation and fecundity to disease and distortion. The work is both humorous and disturbing. Saunders continues to mine this theme in a work titled *The Whirlwind is in the Thorn Bush: Conquest* (2017). In this piece, the ball or 'growth' has expanded to break the fragile back of the Louis XVI-style gilt-wood settee – the irrational and alien conquering the functional.

Nina Saunders, *The Age of Reason*, 1995

Saunders' reuse of pre-existing or found domestic objects can be seen in the context of other established Surrealist practices, particularly the interrogation of commodity fetishism. The Surrealists were interested in outmoded commodities and structures of consumption, as is demonstrated by their preoccupation with arcades, mannequins and shop windows. For the Surrealists, these vestiges of the nineteenth-century consumer economy signalled a distinct set of concerns, revealing the 'ruinous effects of modernisation', as Hal Foster has observed, but they also supplied an imagery that re-entered the commercial sphere 'Surrealised'. The mannequin, for instance, invested with a new range of meanings through Surrealism, became a conduit for the transmission of Surrealist aesthetics within the commercial sphere. In Saunders' *Conquest*, the furniture forms carry with them their historical associations, such as the aristocratic allure of Louis XVI gilt-wood, but are then manipulated with new layers of meaning or narrative. The process of reusing existing objects becomes an active agent in creating narrative in Saunders' work. In her words:

> *I have quite a collection of objects. I feel there is something unique, emotional and urgent about my collection of objects, (something resonates with me), they are the ideas, they sit and wait till I know what it is. ... I source the objects from street corners, auctions, secondhand shops, flea-markets, places all filled to the brim with stories, experiences and musty smells.*[2]

2 'Meet the Artist | Nina Saunders', Hang-Up Gallery Editorial (24 September 2018), https://hanguppictures.com/editorial/meet-the-artist-nina-saunders [Accessed 20 July 2022].

By creating multi-referential juxtapositions through the manipulation and reconfiguring of existing objects, Saunders shifts our relationship with the work, enabling us to develop our own new narratives and stories in response.

Many of the thematic preoccupations of Surrealism allowed for a complex exchange of ideas and imagery between the worlds of art and commerce, and this is particularly true of the body and the imagery of the corporeal. The representation of the body and bodily function became a particular site for Surrealist experiment. It was the subject of intense scrutiny: the body was dismembered, fragmented, eroticised and eulogised in the pursuit of a range of psychological and sexual concerns. In her work, Saunders explores the corporeal with a range of Surrealist strategies. Her use of taxidermy, the melding of dismembered animals with furniture forms, not only recalls the hybrid animal objects and imagery of Carrington and Oppenheim, but also establishes object types that intensively explore the idea of the anthropomorphic. Equally, her melting furniture stresses the corporeal, with its imagery of deformation and degradation caused by what are apparently leaking bodily fluids. Women Surrealists often created works that redesigned or reconfigured the body, playing with its representation as unstable or made of parts recombined in fanciful ways. The body was often transmuted to another state, creating

Nina Saunders, *Wild Swan*, 2019

corporeal imagery that was rooted in deeply subjective
fantasies. Like Saunders, the American surrealist Dorothea
Tanning's *Rainy-Day Canapé* (1970) and *Nue Couchée*
(1969-70) are examples of soft sculptures that explore the
erotic melding of objects and bodies. These works create
unexpected encounters, subverting traditional notions of
both sculpture and furniture. Like Saunders' work, they
fuse the corporeal with ideas of the inanimate.

Gitta Gschwendtner, *Uncanny Lamps*, 2002

Gitta Gschwendtner is a contemporary designer who also plays with notions of the corporeal in Surrealism, examining the idea of an animate 'living' object. In her exhibition *Furniture Life* from 2009, she featured a series of pieces that expressed the idea of injury or damage. Consisting of found and antique works, with the addition of glass elements, these objects appeared to bleed or spill their innards. Her *Hugging Lamps*, initially developed for an exhibition entitled *Uncanny Room*, again suggest the animate. The traditional pleated lampshade is reshaped to encircle or 'hug', as if the lamps are sentient objects able to move, feel and adapt to their surroundings. She continued this theme with a design for a shade that tips up a wall, as if trying to climb to escape its plane. Fusing the corporeal and the emotive, these objects speak to the legacy of Surrealism.

These works also relate to a strand of Surrealist practice that restructured the body's relationship with organic form: the biomorphic. Surrealism provided alternative models to rationalist approaches to design, particularly through the use of nature and natural forms. Nature offered a store of motifs and forms that were quickly adapted for use in design. From the *objets trouvés* (found objects) and automatic techniques that explored chance processes (such as *frottage* and *decalcomania*) to the formal development of biomorphism as an organic form language, Surrealism provided rich and varied new imagery. Nature could represent the Surrealist idea of the marvellous, both in its 'primitivism' and as a metaphorical model for progress. This new currency of meaning, coupled with the formal development of biomorphism as an aesthetic strand, led to the adoption of an organic form language by many artists and designers in the 1930s. The curvilinear biomorphic forms resembling plants or amoeba first developed by German-French sculptor Jean Arp were quickly absorbed into all fields of design, and provided an alternative to the reductive aesthetic of rationalist Modernism. Biomorphic form has remained an aesthetic strand within design discourses. Saunders' deeply organic reconfiguring of furniture that pools, melts and is literally fused with the animal can be seen in the context of Surrealism's investigation of nature and the rich new thread of imagery it provided. Like the organic chair in Leonora Carrington's *The Old Maids*, which metaphorically seats the body in nature, Saunders' furniture transposes the body to an alternate state.

Saunders' work reveals the 'marvellous' – what Surrealist artist Max Ernst referred to as the chance meeting of two distant realities on an unsuitable plane, in a paraphrase of the Comte de Lautréamont's famous expression; it was a formulation that Ernst later simplified to 'systematic estrangement'. The feeling of estrangement or *dépaysement* is evoked in Saunders' designs as she manipulates common and often banal objects to create uncomfortable new dialogues that address a host of themes, from remembrance and loss to the bizarre and humorous. It could hardly be clearer that her strategies sit within the lineage of Surrealism. ■■■■

left Salvador Dalí, Bracelli standing lamp, 2019 edition of 1937 design
below Antoni Gaudí, Armchair for Casa Calvet, Barcelona, Spain, 1975 edition of 1900 design

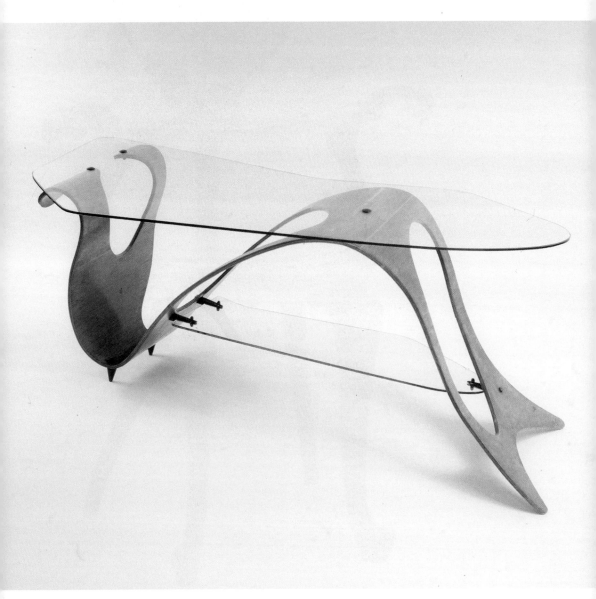

left Carlo Mollino, Tea Table, c.1949
above Salvador Dalí sitting in a functionalist chair before the painting *Inaugural Gooseflesh* at Portlligat, Spain, c.1931

Monkton House, West Sussex, England, 1987. View of the dining room

Dalí's startlingly bold and erotic concept for the Mae West Lips sofa came from a suggestion by his friend and patron, Edward James. James commissioned a sofa inspired by Dalí's gouache painting, *Mae West's Face which may be used as a Surrealist Apartment* (1935). Only five sofas were manufactured. James positioned two next to the Champagne lamps in his home, Monkton House, which had a Surrealist interior-design scheme.

below Edward James and Norris Wakefield for DS Mann, footprint carpet design, c.1930s

Surrealist patron Edward James commissioned this carpet woven with the footprints of his wife, the dancer Tilly Losch. It was inspired by a trail of wet footprints she left after stepping from her bath and captures her fleeting, erotic presence. After the couple divorced, James commissioned another carpet woven with his dog's paw prints, which he said 'represented a more faithful friend'.

right Monkton House, West Sussex, England, 1987. View of the bedroom gallery

above Le Corbusier, Carlos de Beistegui's apartment, Paris, 1929-31. View of the rooftop garden
right Le Corbusier, Carlos de Beistegui's apartment, Paris, 1929. Drawing of the rooftop garden

Le Corbusier was among the first designers to engage with Surrealist ideas and aesthetics. The design of this Parisian apartment shows him combining his signature minimalist architectural lines with a decorative scheme that is opulent and theatrical. The rooftop terrace featured a fantastical open-air fireplace and an empty mirror frame, drawing attention to monuments in the cityscape beyond.

Le Corbusier, Carlos de Beistegui's apartment, Paris, 1929-31. Views of the rooftop garden

top Carlo Mollino, Casa Devalle I, Turin, 1939. Detail of the handle of the mirrored door
bottom Carlo Mollino, Casa Devalle II, Turin, 1940. View of the bedroom
right Carlo Mollino, Casa Devalle I, Turin, 1949. View of the interior

Italian designer and architect Carlo Mollino began to design interiors that reflected the visual language of
Surrealism in the late 1930s. He followed designs by Dalí published in the Surrealist magazine *Minotaure*.
His work featured trompe l'œil effects, bizarre object fragments, padded walls and even a lips-shaped sofa
for the Casa Devalle in Turin that referenced Dalí's Mae West Lips sofa for Monkton House in Sussex, England.

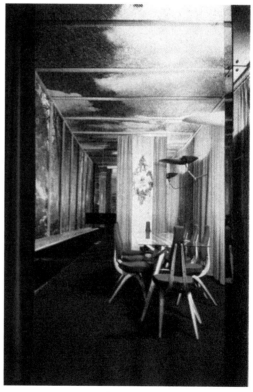

left Carlo Mollino, Casa Rivetti, Turin, 1949. View of the interior
top Carlo Mollino, Casa Rivetti, Turin, 1949. View of the bedroom
bottom Carlo Mollino, Casa Rivetti, Turin, 1949. View of the interior

left Jasper Morrison, Handlebar Table, 1982
below Fernando and Humberto Campana, Cartoon Chair, c.2007

Meret Oppenheim, Traccia (Table with Bird's Feet), 1939

Front, Horse Lamp, 2006

below Gaetano Pesce, Up Chair, 1969

This iconic foam chair, sometimes called 'La Mamma', might look curvy and comforting yet Pesce had a darker, feminist vision. 'It's an image of a prisoner,' he said, referring to the soft ball and chain. 'Women suffer because of the prejudice of men. The chair was supposed to talk about this problem.'

right Nanda Vigo, Due più (Two more), 1971

Vigo's pioneering practice was characterised by bold and sensual combinations of material and form that ask to be touched and experienced. She often combined hard and soft textures, such as glass or metal and fake fur. These unusual stools were created for a coffee shop in Milan. For another interior-design commission, Vigo covered an entire spiral staircase with fake fur, leaving only the upper treads bare.

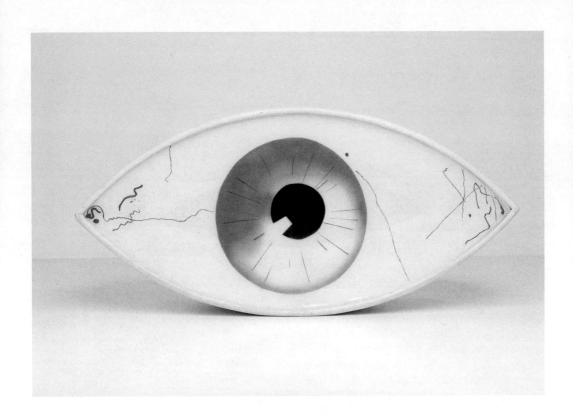

above Man Ray, Le Témoin (The Witness), 1971. Paradisoterrestre Edition, 2020

Radically conceptual, the 1971 Ultramobile furniture collection was made in collaboration with Surrealist artists including Meret Oppenheim, Roberto Sebastian Matta and Man Ray. Dino Gavina, founder of Simon International, described the collection as 'a presence that pulsates and breathes in your home'. Although a sculpture, Le Témoin can be flipped on its side to function as a sofa or low table.

right Robert Stadler, Pools & Pouf!, 2004

Humberto Campana — who works with his brother Fernando as São Paulo-based design duo Estudio Campana — was interviewed by Priya Khanchandani, Head of Curatorial and Interpretation at the Design Museum. After making their name as furniture designers in 1984, Estudio Campana have produced major architectural projects and scenography for ballet, and collaborated with fashion brands. Their work is in the permanent collections of cultural institutions worldwide.

ESTUDIO CAMPANA

&

PRIYA KHANCHANDANI

PK Let's focus first on a particular object we are showing in the exhibition: the Cabana cabinet. It's a very distinctive object, with a mysterious quality. When you encounter it, you see a waterfall of raffia and you might not perceive it as a cabinet. Was it your intention to introduce mystery to what is otherwise quite a pragmatic piece of design?

HC Yes, I wanted to construct an object that connected to spirituality and shamanism, and bring all these elements from Brazilian and African religions into this object. What is it? Is it a cabinet or is it a sculpture? Once you open it, you can hide things inside. I try to put soul and life into all the objects I create. It's important to me to put meaning and life into them, so that they don't rest silently in people's rooms. Objects call for attention, they have to catch your eye and they have to look like living beings.

PK That's a very beautiful way of describing objects. In some ways, the Cabana cabinet is the counterpoint to Modernism, which is about functionality, with the essence of the purpose of the object being at the forefront. Do you think the experimentation inherent in Surrealism has liberated your work from the boundaries of Modernism?

HC First of all, Brazil is very surreal — it's crazy to live here! You know that 1980s movie *Brazil*? It's by a British director [Terry Gilliam, *Brazil*, 1985]. Well, life here is exactly like in that movie ... it's chaos. We have such a rich popular culture, so diverse, and because of the dimensions of the country we have different elements from south to north and from east to west. So Brazil is not a Modernist country; even though we have Brasília, which was constructed by Oscar Niemeyer, the people and the roots are very anti-Modernism. Brazil is colourful, noisy and very hybrid, with Indigenous, African, Portuguese, Asian and Lebanese elements. I try to put all these aspects of Brazilian culture into my work.

Fernando and Humberto Campana, Cabana cabinet, 2003

PK Do you think that Brazilian design has a different relationship with Surrealism than Western design?

HC I can see a connection to Surrealism in mine and my brother's work, because we always speak about dreams and fantasies: we are storytellers. Even to this day, I still question what I am. Am I a designer or an artist? I don't care to know, but I have the passion to create my experiences and to show my emotions.

PK I like the idea of storytelling — that comes across powerfully. This takes us to the other object from the exhibition which has a strong storytelling aspect: the Cartoon Chair, a chair upholstered with Disney toys. In your work, you often use found materials and reinvent them in playful ways. What is it about found objects that you find intriguing?

HC I love the idea of giving a second life to an already existing element, like chairs made from tubes, or plushies in this case, and my brother and I always wanted to create furniture using traditional methods of upholstery. One day there was a guy walking in front of our studio selling plush toys, carrying some on his head. The image was so beautiful that I looked to my brother and said, 'This could be a chair!' So we bought the whole bunch of toys from the guy. There were alligators, lions, teddy bears and many more. Then I started stitching one plushie to the other while my brother created the metal structure. We are non-conformist — I like to give value to materials which are discarded, then reuse them. The plushies also reminded me of all the cartoons I saw in my childhood. Years later, Disney UK invited us to create a chair for them, and they gave us total freedom to use whichever character we wanted. We always loved Mickey Mouse, as he is so playful, and with his big ears he is a very Surrealist character.

Fernando and Humberto Campana, Cartoon Chair, c.2007

PK The idea of using characters who are ubiquitous and so recognisable was such an interesting choice. Were you conscious that they should be recognisable characters, and how did you want people to relate to them?

HC I never really thought about this. I usually jump very wildly into an idea, once I recognise it's a good one. The only thing I really think about is how I am going to construct the object. I always try to use the eyes of a child and to create as if I were in kindergarten. I never think of the reaction people could have; I only think of solving my problems, metaphysical or emotional.

PK The use of a consumerist product, like the Disney toys, within the context of furniture is a surreal gesture, but it also implies an interesting relationship with postmodernism. I don't know whether you think in these terms, but how would you situate your work between Surrealism and postmodernism?

HC I never studied art, I must confess, but these two movements match. Mickey Mouse is a kind of reaction to consumerism, rationalism and the way to construct, like postmodernism and Surrealism. I recognise my work as connected to Surrealism and postmodernism, but completely by chance. I loved Salvador Dalí and Fellini: they were my icons. There was a cartoon made by Disney and designed by Dalí, which is so beautiful. They were my icons: Salvador, Picasso and the Tropicalism movement — all people who reacted to rationalism and consumerism.

Fernando and Humberto Campana, Cartoon Chair, c.2007

PK When you talk about the interaction between consumer culture and art, it makes me think of your idea of 'contamination': you once said 'our work is about contamination, as much as the world contaminates ourselves we want to contaminate the world'. What were you referring to, and were you talking about the breaking down of barriers between high and low culture?

HC Part of our work is intended to bring hope, and you can create objects yourself using your eyes. To make a better world, working with your hands is very important because it brings love to the object. I try to look for things in the hidden corners of society, and I try to cast a light on to things that people might not see. I try to transform something very banal into something precious, and by doing this I create a contamination because people start to think differently — like we did with the Favela Chair, which is a wooden chair made with discarded pieces of wood. I think it is a good example of why people think that things need to be very rational, when there is a better way to construct things, through contamination.

Fernando and Humberto Campana, Favela Chair, 1991

PK This idea of reclaiming and reconfiguring found materials in unexpected ways was an ingredient of Radical Design, but it seems that it was drawing from Brazilian design culture as well. Do you think that's fair? Or, if not, where did that way of working come from?

HC Yes, most of our pieces are based on Brazilian culture. Brazil is fertile soil for everything. Life here is constantly changing and we always need to be prepared for the next step. It is a country that has no stability, and you need to be very sharp and clever to survive here. Mine and my brother's work is very much based on Brazilian culture, and we are of Italian descent but we have Portuguese, African and Indigenous influences in our blood, and we carry all these elements into our work. I also try to be honest when I create an object. I always ask myself, 'Am I copying someone?' Today it is so difficult, because communication happens so quickly, but I try to stay close to my roots.

PK What is the legacy of Surrealism in your work, and is it still something you turn to as a point of inspiration?

HC For me, it is. I love dreams. I love to get out of this planet — life is so boring here. My antennae and my head are constantly searching for dreams to get out of ordinary life, and, in that sense, this is Surrealism. I also try to connect to spiritualism and to shamanism. I've been working on this collection based on vernacular culture that connects to shamanism, to the earth, to terracotta, and to all these elements from Indigenous and African cultures here in Brazil.

PK Do you think Surrealism will continue to be relevant to design more broadly?

HC Yes, of course. Surrealism will never stop being relevant, because dreams will always be present in people's lives. Surrealism will be constantly moving and changing, but it will still be Surrealism.

PK Are you more interested in Surrealist sources from past times, or are you finding new sources of Surrealism in the contemporary? For example, are you still looking at Dalí and the greats, or has that changed?

HC Yes, it has definitely changed, because we have Instagram and movies that are easily accessible. My eyes are always looking for all the information that I can get and the things I can recognise in someone's work. I am always looking for something. Yes, there was Dalí and Schiaparelli — but now there are so many artists working in Surrealism, and so many things happening with digital technology, and I am constantly looking for other possibilities. ▬

AL

CRAFTS

Jonathan Trayte, *Lunar Camel (1&2)*, 2022

STRANGE BEDFELLOWS: ON CRAFT & SURREALISM

Craft, on the face of it, is everything Surrealism is not. It is above all pragmatic: a way of getting things done in the tangible world. This demands both investment in skill and a basis in thoughtful intention. These necessities would seem antithetical to Surrealism's preoccupations with the unconscious, and with procedures such as the *objet trouvé* (or 'found object') and chance operations. Philosophically, too, the two would seem to be directly opposed. Craft embodies cultural continuity, rooted in modest community values. Surrealism – at least in its initial incarnation – was libertine, self-permissive, something dreamed up to shock.

Strange, then, that Surrealism has been one of the dominant aesthetic modes of the Studio Craft movement since 1945, and still exerts a powerful influence on contemporary independent design today. In disciplines like ceramics, glass, furniture, jewellery and textiles, the imprint of Surrealism far exceeds that of avant-garde movements like Cubism, Constructivism and even Bauhaus-inspired functionalism – all of which one might have expected to be far more congenial to the

Harvey Littleton, *Implosion / Explosion*, 1964

progressive-minded artisan. So pervasive has this influence been that craft has been a sort of game preserve for Surrealist form, carrying on that line of experimental thinking to an extent unmatched in other disciplines, with the possible exceptions of fashion and photography.

One simple explanation for this surprising state of affairs is that modern craftspeople have embraced Surrealism as a means of subverting expectations. The modern potter or weaver is beset by constraining notions of tradition, utility and 'good form'. What better response than to seek out the improbable, to unseat convention? From this point of view, Surrealism is a box of odd tools, which can be used to dismantle a craft discipline from within.

Exhibit A, in this account, would be a work like Harvey Littleton's *Implosion/Explosion*. It was made in 1964, during the early, experimental years of the American glass revival, when makers were coming to grips with just about everything in their craft all at once – furnace design, batch formulation, forming techniques, you name it. That difficult struggle shows in *Implosion/Explosion*, one side of which has exploded outward. Littleton could well have considered it an outright failure, albeit a dramatic one, and simply discarded it. Yet, as his metaphorical title implies, he was able to see something exciting in the way that the glass sought its own escape route. With eyes conditioned to the Surrealist paradigm and its embrace of the aleatory, Littleton could admire the suggestive opening of the amoeboid shape, like a three-dimensional Rorschach blot; the red discolouration of the greenish factory glass, which suggests a pair of luridly painted lips; the wonderful wrongness of it all.

Such examples only take us so far, however. If all that Surrealism offered to craft was arbitrary contradiction and happy accident, it would scarcely have appealed to so many different kinds of makers over so many decades. The real potential of Surrealism for craft was what happened when it was embraced *without* the sacrifice of skill, complex materiality and historic resonance: embraced in such a way as to create tension with traditional canons of workmanship, yes, but also to mobilise latent possibilities in Surrealism that would never have occurred to the movement's originators.

This is what we see in Marvin Lipofsky's *California Loops* series, for example, made a few years after Littleton's *Implosion/Explosion*, just as the counterculture was cresting on the West Coast. Psychedelia was in the air and, with it,

Marvin Lipofsky, *California Loops Series #32*, 1969

a new relevance for Surrealist ideas. The suggestive shape of the blown glass – not quite sexual, but nonetheless provocative – is heightened by the unexpected addition of flocking, a soft texture somewhat akin to Meret Oppenheim's famous *non sequitur* of a fur-lined teacup.

Lipofsky's work also exemplifies the Studio Craft movement's embrace of biomorphism, an idiom developed by the first-generation Surrealists – Arp, Masson, Miró, Tanguy – as a way to suggest organic growth outside the dominion of reason. For them, biomorphism was 'the analogue of manic activity in the artist', as Lawrence Alloway memorably put it, 'whose muscular activity issues in the marks which we interpret as a self-discovering subject'.[1] It was meant to be wholly adventitious, like automatic writing, a way to free the artist's mind and let primal urges spill right into the work.

When transposed into the disciplines of craft, however, biomorphism took on a very different character. In making a drawing, or even when sawing and bending plywood (as Ray Eames did in her sculptures of the 1940s), one can let a line wander, allow a shape to define itself more or less in the moment. But it was another matter entirely to make biomorphic blown glass; or to hammer metal into rippling, overlapping contours, like the Greenwich Village jewellers Sam Kramer and Art Smith; or to glue up stacks of boards and carve them into monumental yet sinuous furniture, like Wendell Castle; or to weave abstractions, like those of Magdalena Abakanowicz, which reinterpreted the idea of biomorphism along suggestively gendered lines. Despite the immediacy of all these works, it obviously required considerable forethought to arrive at such sophisticated compositions. The simple fact of time – the extended duration necessary for the planning and execution of the works – invalidated any possibility of interpreting them as the direct upwelling of the unconscious.

Such objects are sometimes classed within the category of 'organic design', an idiom codified by the Museum of Modern Art in 1941, and summarised by designer Eva Zeisel:

1 Lawrence Alloway, 'The Biomorphic '40s', *Artforum* 4/1 (September 1965), 18-22: 19.

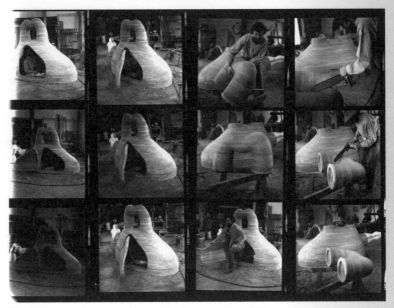

Wendell Castle working on *Environment for Contemplation*, 1969

2 Quoted in Jeffrey L. Meikle, *Design in the USA* (Oxford: Oxford University Press, 2005), 152. See also Brooke Kamin Rapaport, Kevin Stayton et al., *Vital Forms: American Art in the Atomic Age 1940 to 1960* (Brooklyn: Brooklyn Museum of Art, 2001).

'modern tables, containers, and all sorts of things suddenly began to melt, to become soft'.[2] Zeisel herself identified Salvador Dali's *The Persistence of Memory* (1931) as a source for this trend – and a trend it was, a look that could be applied to serially manufactured ceramics and furniture, without any particular Surrealist intent. Studio Craft's explorations of biomorphism should be distinguished from this generic style: they had special significance because of the personal involvement of the maker in the act of creation.

Neither delineated in a fit of absence of mind – as was supposedly the case for the early Surrealists – nor adopted as the latest fashionable silhouette, handmade biomorphism was a uniquely exploratory mode, a way to give visual expression to the idea of 'flow'. This term would not be properly theorised until 1990, in the work of Mihály Csíkszentmihályi, but has been tacitly understood by artisans since human beings first mastered tools.[3] In all that time, no stylistic mode had afforded the compass – quite literally, the wiggle room – that biomorphism does for interaction with materiality as such. When it comes to craft, the devil may be in the details, but so is the pleasure. Biomorphism was the ideal language for individualistic, self-actualised makers: it freed them from

3 Mihály Csíkszentmihályi, *Flow: The Psychology of Optimal Experience* (New York: Harper and Row, 1990).

the usual canons of structure and ornament, allowing them to step into their workshop and then follow their bliss.

A thornier situation altogether is craft's relationship to the Surrealist 'ready-made' or found object, which (as mentioned above) would seem to be the complete antithesis of the artisanal. A Duchampian found object executes a neat end-run around the whole territory of skill, with all its challenges and possibilities. Yet, as the British art theorist John Roberts has argued, the 'ready-made' did not so much invalidate conventional skill as position it within a new dialectical structure – often resulting in what he calls 'reskilling': that is, the introduction of previously unconventional techniques into the making of art.[4]

A quintessential example of this is seen in so-called 'Super Realist' craft, which initially developed in the 1970s, closely paralleled by tendencies in painting and sculpture.[5] As the name suggests, Super Realism was to some extent a revival of Surrealism (the terms are synonymous, both literally meaning 'beyond the actual'), and often arrived at a heightened version of the uncanny effects sought by artists like Oppenheim and Dali. Exquisite workmanship was the norm in the movement; photographic effects were achieved by hand by painters like Richard Estes and Audrey Flack, and sculptors like Duane Hanson.[6]

In ceramics, the feat of legerdemain was arguably even more technically astounding. In both the European and Chinese contexts, the discipline does have a *trompe l'oeil* tradition – tureens that look like cabbages, pots with faux woodgrain – but making clay actually look like leather or metal is no easy trick. California artists like Marilyn Levine and Richard Shaw managed it, though, using precise casting and surface embellishment to render leather bags and coats in stoneware, or sticks, stones and string in porcelain. These were 'handmade ready-mades' (or, in Shaw's case, the 'assisted ready-made' assemblage), in which the deadpan affect of the Duchampian found object was infused with a countervailing mimetic impulse: a will to replicate.

4 John Roberts, *The Intangibilities of Form* (London: Verso, 2007).

5 The key text on the movement remains Gregory Battcock, *Super Realism: A Critical Anthology* (New York: E. P. Dutton, 1975). On ceramics and the movement, see Garth Clark and Margie Hughto, *A Century of Ceramics in the United States, 1878-1978* (New York: E. P. Dutton, 1979).

6 On the relationship of Super Realism to photography, see Ralph Rugoff, *The Painting of Everyday Life: 1960s to Now* (London: Hayward Gallery, 2007).

Wendell Castle, *Ghost Clock*, 1985

It was Wendell Castle who contributed the undoubted masterwork of Super Realist craft: his 1985 *Ghost Clock*, now the beloved centrepiece of the Renwick Gallery in Washington, D.C. The culmination of an ongoing investigation into *trompe l'oeil* carving, the work looks for all the world like a 'ready-made' – a grandfather clock under a dust cover – but is in fact carved from solid mahogany, partly bleached to mimic white fabric (the woodgrain shows through, a purposeful telltale at close range). Though it is often noted that the work cleverly alludes to the drapery of a classical statue, its eerie, quasi-figural presence is really closer to that of paintings by René Magritte such as *The Lovers* (1928), which shows a couple kissing, their heads completely shrouded.

As *Ghost Clock* powerfully demonstrates, craft artists found numerous ingenious ways to breathe new life into Surrealism, adapting its iconography and tactics to suit their own particular purposes. Even over the past two decades, as the Studio Craft movement has passed gradually into history, independent designers have followed suit. They do not tend to identify themselves with a single material, nor engage directly with an artisanal tradition (either in a spirit of fidelity or of disruption).[7] These new designers do, however, remain committed to the expressive reinvention of making processes – and also to the legacy of Surrealism.

The polymorphous works of London-based designer Jonathan Trayte pick up where Super Realism left off. He opened his own studio following stints as a chef and then as a professional fabricator. That background shows in his work, which is built from numerous materials but

7 See Glenn Adamson, 'The Three Pillars of Design', *Design Edit* (8 November 2021), https://thedesignedit. com/the-three-pillars- of-design/ [accessed 30 June 2022].

8 Q&A with Jonathan Trayte in *MelonMelon-Tangerine* (New York: Friedman Benda, 2021), https://issuu.com/kate1414/docs/trayte_mmt [accessed 30 June 2022].

assumes the form of ripe fruits and vegetables, somewhat like the allegorical figures of sixteenth-century painter Giuseppe Arcimboldo (which were beloved of the Surrealists). Trayte has spoken of his desire to stage palpable oppositions in his imagery – 'absurd, but also descriptive ... edible and delicious, but also repulsive' – a range of effects that he achieves through his superlative control of materials and surface finishes.[8]

The Netherlands-based design duo Odd Matter (Els Woldhek and Georgi Manassiev) are yet more explicit in their commitment to a maximalist form of Surrealism, asserting that 'nothing not super can be tolerated. The only way to a super house is freak honesty as no common or widely accepted view would be able to deliver a true extreme.'[9] The objects in their Guise collection, made from carved EPS (expanded polystyrene) foam and surfaced either in sprayed auto lacquers or scagliola (faux marbling), look like special effects, broken loose from a screen near you. As the title Guise indicates, Odd Matter are concerned here with the play of appearances, but also of agency and identity. They are updating biomorphism for the age of artificial intelligence, toying with the question of what forms taken from life might mean, when life is itself being reinvented. If there is a 'self-discovering subject' here (to recall Lawrence Alloway's description of Surrealist method), it may be one that is escaping the bounds of the merely human.

9 Q&A with Odd Matter, *Superhouse* (2020), www.superhouse.us/artists-designers/odd-matter [accessed 30 June 2022].

If and when craft's special relationship with Surrealism does come to an end, it will probably be at the ghostly hands of virtual technology. The metaverse (another term that is etymologically parallel to the Surreal) is opening up vast new landscapes of the possible, populated by born-digital objects that may or may not ultimately find themselves incarnated in physical form. In this brave new world, will craft find yet another means of reinventing itself? Will makers discover new languages and methodologies as generative as those that Surrealism bequeathed to them in the twentieth century? Only time will tell. If so, it will be because they still dare to dream. ▬▬▬▬

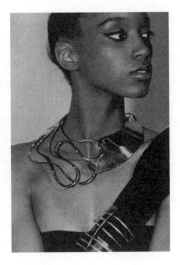

top left Art Smith, Ellington necklace and Baker cuff, c.1962
top right Art Smith, Half and Half necklace and Modern cuff, 1948
bottom Art Smith, Lava bracelet, 1946

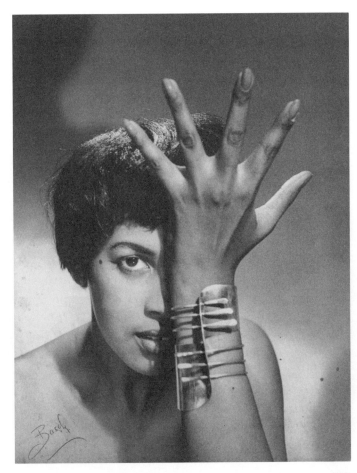

Art Smith, Paramecium necklace, c.1955

above Odd Matter, Guise table, 2019
right Odd Matter, Guise table lamp, 2019

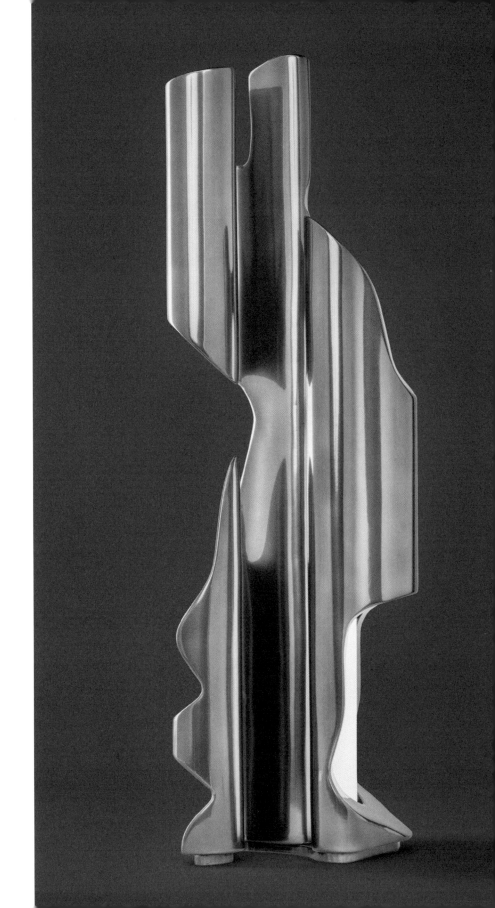

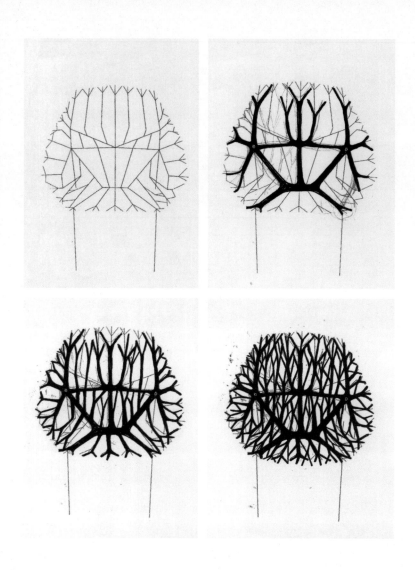

Ronan & Erwan Bouroullec, drawings for Vegetal Chair, 2004-8

The early Surrealists found inspiration for alternative and original creative approaches in natural forms and organic processes of growth. In a similar vein, Ronan and Erwan Bouroullec set out to create a chair that would 'sprout up like a plant'. It took them four years to develop a design that was both poetic and robust, with the aid of advanced plastic-injection-moulding techniques and virtual-modelling software.

Ronan & Erwan Bouroullec, Vegetal Chair, 2004-8

Konstantin Grcic, *Coathangerbrush*, 1992

Transforming everyday objects by placing them in new and surprising combinations is a Surrealist strategy. Fantasy and functionality co-exist in Grcic's design, in which a coat hanger can also be used as a clothes brush. Grcic is inspired by Magritte, who, he says, 'looks at the world and unhinges it … [his] Surrealist images are actually about reality'.

Bless, BLESSbeauty Hairbrush, 1999

Ingo Maurer, Luzy pendant, 2018

left Ingo Maurer, *Porca Miseria!*, 1994

Broken with a hammer or dropped on the floor, ceramics have been shattered into hundreds of pieces to create this chandelier. Maurer painstakingly reassembled the shards to capture the moment of fragmentation and the form created by chance. The title of this work is an Italian exclamation of dismay or wonder.

Jean Lurçat, *Jeu d'Artifice*, 1966

French artist Jean Lurçat created tapestries that draw on Surrealist influences. Often featuring verses by Surrealist poets Paul Éluard and Robert Desnos, the tapestries also suggest fantastical worlds where mystical creatures roam through nature and the cosmos. Lurçat exhibited alongside Surrealist artists from 1925, but never considered himself a member of the movement.

above Jonathan Trayte, *Lunar Camel (1&2)*, 2022
right Jonathan Trayte, *Pink Hot Solar Buzzer*, 2019

Audrey Large, *TP-TS-112.Mocap*, 2018

Large challenges our perception of what is real with works that sit at the boundary of digital design and handcrafts. She translates digital images into improbable physical forms using techniques including modelling and 3D printing.

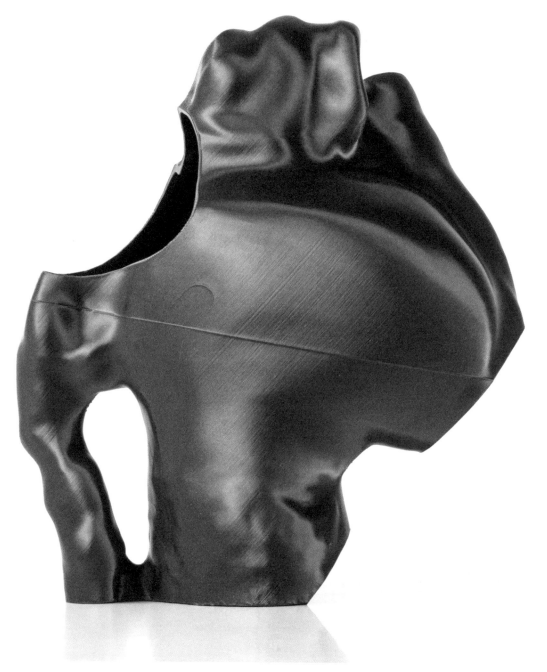

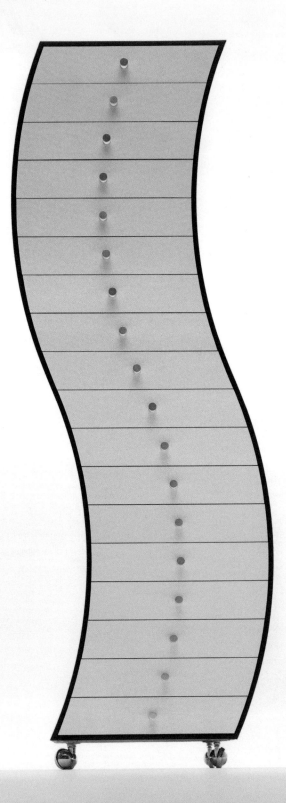

right Nacho Carbonell, *Lily Pad Tree,* 2018

This fantastical object sparks the imagination. Like earlier artists and designers working with Surrealist ideas, Carbonell transforms everyday materials into strange, animated new forms. His projects often start with leftover scraps of material in the studio, which are then reconfigured and assembled in surprising ways.

bottom Jürgen Bey, *Tree Trunk Bench,* 1999

This fantastical bench is completed by a locally sourced tree trunk or planks. Bey's design combines this natural object with culture and tradition, represented by the three cast-bronze chair backs that are wedged into the tree trunk.

left Salvador Dalí and Edward James, Cat's Cradle Hands Chair, c.1936
below Pedro Friedeberg, Hand Chair, 1962

left Gjon Mili, Vallauris, France, 1949. Pablo Picasso drawing with light
above Front, Sketch Furniture, c.2014
right Front, Sketch Furniture, AP 2, 2015

Sketch furniture is traced by the designer's hand and body in mid-air using motion-capture technology. The forms are translated into a digital file and 3D printed to create functional pieces. Design studio Front innovated this method in 2005 to introduce instinct and physicality into the design process. Their gestures recall Picasso's much earlier experiments in 'drawing' with light as well as Surrealist processes such as automatic writing.

Dunne & Raby were in conversation with Kathryn Johnson, Design Museum curator of the exhibition *Objects of Desire: Surrealism and Design 1924 – Today*. Since the 1990s, Anthony Dunne's and Fiona Raby's design practice – informed by shared interests in science, art, technology and literature – has centred on critical design. In the early 2000s, they pioneered the new practice of speculative design, developing objects that speak to speculative futures and act as catalysts for the design imagination. Dunne & Raby are professors of design and emerging technology at The New School in New York.

DUNNE & RABY

&

KATHRYN JOHNSON

KJ It's nine years since the publication of *Speculative Everything: Design, Fiction and Social Dreaming*, your brilliant survey of speculative design practice in the wake of the 2008 financial crash. At that time, you contrasted standard design practice, 'A', with speculative design practice, 'B', and looked ahead to 'C, D and E', too. How have C, D and E taken shape since then?

D&R There have been several C, D and E's by other people. We're currently working on 'C/D: Designing in Paradoxical Times', in which we borrow some ideas from

DOGMA	>	DOUBT
NEW NORMALS	>	POST NORMAL
EXTRAPOLATION	>	PARALLELISM
KNOWN UNKNOWNS	>	UNKNOWN UNKNOWNS
SCIENCE FICTION	>	EXTRO-SCIENCE FICTION
REAL WORLD	>	MANY REALS
PROTOTYPE	>	MODEL
NEWTONIAN MECHANICS	>	QUANTUM MECHANICS
UTOPIA / DYSTOPIA	>	HETEROTOPIA
ALTERNATIVE FUTURES	>	ALTERNATIVE WORLDVIEWS
EITHER/ OR	>	AND/ BOTH
VISION	>	THOUGHT EXPERIMENT
UNIVERSE	>	FRACTIVERSE
FICTION VS REALITY	>	A LARGER REALITY
POSSIBLE OBJECTS	>	IMPOSSIBLE OBJECTS

Dunne & Raby, C/D: Designing in Paradoxical Times, 2020

Quentin Meillassoux (extro-science fiction), John Law (reals, fractiverse), Ursula K Le Guin (larger reality) and Ziauddin Sardar (postnormal times). We're also in the middle of a new book project and much of it touches on tensions between the real and the unreal, and what this might mean for design.

We previously felt that unreality — the space outside all the probable, possible and potential realities we discussed in *Speculative Everything* — was unproductive. Now we feel that this is exactly where we need to be looking. Unlike the other models of the future, which all lead back to the present and are therefore versions of it, the external realm offers a space of genuinely fluid exploration. But it means engaging with the unreal, and being constructively unrealistic. To do this, it is necessary to embrace new ways of thinking that break with conventional design wisdom and begin to experiment with other kinds of wisdom, much of which may feel counter-intuitive or even unpalatable in the context of design. Surrealism, for example.

KJ You've written of the importance of 'loosening reality's grip on the imagination'. This reminded me of André Breton's 1924 *Manifesto of Surrealism*, where he writes that the imagination 'paces back and forth in a cage'. Do you think the Surrealist inward focus on individual dreams and psychology remains important in 2022?

D&R We believe our inner and social worlds are linked and work together. And both need attention. If our inner worlds become depleted, which we feel is happening at the moment, then social dreaming and the collective imagination will suffer too. As designers, we are trained to focus on the world out there, but our inner worlds need nourishment as well.

The kind of design we are engaged in has several purposes: to nourish the worlds we carry around inside us, to prompt thinking about alternative ways of being in the present world, and to provide new vantage points that allow for a questioning of assumptions and values. One of the challenges here, though, is to ensure that forays into unreality are temporary rather than permanent.

KJ How do you try to keep things constructive and temporary, as you say, in your work?

Dunne & Raby, *Designs for an overpopulated planet:
The Foragers*, 2009

D&R It's something we grapple with all the
time, especially in our teaching. It's hard
to say precisely how we impose limits and
make sure our ideas are helpful. Maybe this
is where the craft in speculative forms of
design lies. Rather than linking ideas back
to the present, we encourage our students
to leap into an imagined world based on
their ongoing interests or research. They
develop a set of values, belief systems,
cosmologies or worldviews that are
fictional. When materialised as words or
everyday objects that mirror existing ones
— transport systems, clothing, furniture,
technology or even legal documents
such as constitutions — they create a
very productive space for developing
new perspectives on the existing situation.
Rather than trying to find solutions,
we develop 'useful fictions' that provide
tools for thinking with.

KJ Could you tell me more about your
interest in science fiction and literature?
It seems that experiments with words
often precede new directions in
visual culture and design, Surrealism
being one example of this.

D&R Over the years, our interest has shifted
from straightforward science fiction that
explores the implications of new technologies,
often extrapolating from the present situation,
to fiction that plays with more philosophical
ideas. One of the key techniques we make
use of is 'cognitive estrangement', a term
coined by Darko Suvin in the 1970s to
describe how sci-fi can act as a foil against
which we can compare our own reality
and engage with it more critically. This is
something we try to do in our design work:
making use of different kinds of wrongness,
for example, to engage the viewer.

Since writing *Speculative Everything*,
we've seen design futures and design
speculation converge. We're finding that
when we design for the 'not here, not now',
our work is by default relocated to a 'future'
— particularly if technology is involved. But
futures are just one way of framing the not
here and not now; they're not always helpful
for the kind of work we do. In contrast to
futurology, future studies and foresight —
which all attempt to mitigate risk in the face of
uncertainty, or to identify preferred futures —
the future's primary value for us is a place for
thought experiments that explore alternative
values and worldviews made concrete
through the design of everyday things.

The futures we carry around inside
us have also become colonised by the
technological dreams of the entertainment
and technology industries, so that the future

Dunne & Raby, *Designs for an overpopulated planet:
The Foragers*, 2009

as a concept for facilitating imaginative thought has become too restrictive. If, besides nourishing the worlds we carry around inside us, the purpose of designing for worlds that do not exist is to prompt thinking about alternative ways of being in the present world, then we might need to move beyond futures as the primary way of doing this.

The interesting issue for us is how speculative forms of design practice complement work being done in other fields. Design materialises only small parts of fictional worlds, unlike architecture or science-fiction cinema where whole cities and worlds can be represented. Maybe this fragmentary approach creates more room for the viewer's imagination. Perhaps the special quality that design brings to the conversation around fiction and technology is a more suggestive and open-ended approach. But compared with literature and even architecture, where speculative forms of thought have existed for centuries, it's still early days for design.

KJ I'm interested in how you position objects in relation to texts in your work. Is there a functional difference, or is it messier than that?

D&R Words and objects allow us to explore ideas from different angles — as do drawings. Many of our projects start with conversations between the two of us or are inspired by ideas we encounter in books. In that sense, words are an integral part of what we do. It's just that sometimes they lead us to design objects, and at other times to write more words. So, the answer is that it's messy!

While curating a section of *Exemplary: 150 years of the MAK from Arts and*

Crafts to Design with Thomas Geisler, which took place at the MAK in Vienna in 2014, our contribution sparked a very lively debate about the form in which the text-based objects we had selected for display could be acquired for the museum collection. In the end, they were accepted as modified physical books, actual objects, rather than a collection of fictional text-based objects.

This debate led us down the road of 'impossible objects'. Someone mentioned the essay 'Theory of Objects' (1904) by Austrian philosopher Alexius Meinong. According to Meinong, objects as random as actual entities (tables and chairs), non-actual entities (numbers and ideas), fictional entities (Sherlock Holmes, King of France, unicorns), and even impossible objects (e.g. round squares, perpetual-motion machines) all exist on the same plane. Some are physical objects while others are ideas that we share in our collective imagination. But all have an impact on the world and what we think about it.

We also combined text and design in *An Archive of Impossible Objects*, commissioned by the Kunstmuseen in Krefeld, Germany, for display in a house designed by Mies van der Rohe. We designed ten globes referencing imagined worlds in literature, thought experiments by scientists, and conspiracy theories. Each one represents a different way of viewing the world, and reality itself. There are also three speculative topographic maps, suggesting very different forces and conditions from our own planet. These were meant to invite the viewer to speculate further. The objects and drawings were exhibited with links to more online information about the sources of each globe.

Dunny & Raby, *An Archive of Impossible Objects: Globes*, 2018

KJ That was such a beautiful display. I think the online catalogue compared it with a Renaissance *studiolo*, or space for study. Do you think speculative design also has a place outside universities and museums? Where is it happening today?

D&R We're a bit wary of the label 'speculative design' at this stage. We prefer to think about speculative forms of design practice, of which there are many. We are aware of it being used in industry research labs, independent design studios, academic departments and schools, government policy units and even grassroots organisations. Of course, some contexts require more applied approaches than others.

Our project has sought to create more room within design for radically imaginative thought that challenges deeply ingrained assumptions. If you are interested in pushing at the edges of practice, then, like research in any field, this kind of work needs to happen in an environment suited to the exploration and production of new ideas, such as academia. Speculative forms of design practice can give tangible form to complex ideas from fields such as science, the humanities and philosophy, creating bridges between different disciplines, sectors and publics. They can flourish in the research environments of art–and–design colleges and universities, where resources are few and far between, but ideas are abundant. And as with any discipline, there needs to be a dialogue between researchers and practitioners. ▬

FA

PHOTOG

Tilda Swinton, Fashion: Vera Wang, Vicki Beamon. Las Pozas, Mexico, 2012. Photograph by Tim Walker

FASHION

RAPHY

ESSAY **SUSANNA BROWN**

STRANGER
THAN
PARADISE

THE MODERN ARTIST SHOULD PARTICIPATE IN EVERY KIND OF EXTRACURRICULAR ACTIVITY. MICHELANGELO DESIGNED THE DRESS FOR THE POPE'S SWISS GUARDS. IT IS ALL PART OF THE PROPAGANDA OF YOUR IMAGINATION ...
SALVADOR DALÍ [1]

1 Salvador Dalí, quoted in Hannah Crawforth, 'Surrealism and the Fashion Magazine', *American Periodicals*, 14/2 (2004), 212.

2 In 2012, New York's Metropolitan Museum of Art staged the exhibition *Schiaparelli and Prada: Impossible Conversations*, celebrating the affinities between two pioneering Italian women from different eras and revealing new readings of their most innovative designs.

Fashion design and Surrealism have been in dialogue since the 1930s, and practitioners such as Dalí viewed design as a natural extension of their art. Elsa Schiaparelli, the couturière most closely associated with the movement, collaborated with Dalí and created iconic Surreal fashion including the Tear dress, Shoe hat and Bug necklace. Numerous avant-garde artists turned their hand to radical jewellery design, while others painted arresting covers for the fashion magazines *Vogue* and *Harper's Bazaar*. Early fashion photographers incorporated Surrealist tropes and worked closely with artists in the creative melting-pot of pre-war Paris.

Surrealism's influence on dress extends into the twenty-first century through designers including Rei Kawakubo, Martin Margiela, Miuccia Prada and Maria Grazia Chiuri.[2] For Dior's Spring/Summer 2018 haute couture show, Chiuri presented seventy ensembles on a chequerboard set beneath huge plaster casts of eyes, ears and noses suspended from a mirrored ceiling. The collection was inspired by the work of the Argentine Surrealist Leonor Fini and the fabled Bal

Elsa Schiaparelli, Tear dress, 1938

3 The Italian-Argentine Surrealist Leonor Fini had a particular connection to Christian Dior: long before he embarked on a career in fashion, Dior ran a gallery in Paris, at 34 rue de la Boétie, and in 1932 he gave Fini her first solo exhibition in France. The exhibition was held from 24 November to 7 December 1932. Maria Grazia Chiuri turned to the female Surrealists again for Dior's Autumn/Winter 2020 collection, producing an homage to photographers Lee Miller and Dora Maar, and artists Leonora Carrington and Jacqueline Lamba.

Oriental of 1951.³ Fini was one of a thousand special guests who travelled from all over the world to Venice for the ball of the century, hosted by the flamboyant art collector Carlos de Beistegui. A highlight was 'The Ghosts of Venice', a theatrical entrance devised by Dior and Dalí that featured eight characters in spectacular masks and costumes as giants and dwarves – such whimsical splendour had rarely been seen since the court of Louis XIV.

The designers of today fusing Surreal thinking and cutting-edge technology include Daniel Roseberry (artistic director at the recently relaunched house of Schiaparelli), Iris van Herpen and Mary Katrantzou. 'The Surrealist Ideal' was the title of Katrantzou's Autumn/Winter 2012 collection, in which pencils, spoons and typewriters became extraordinary through her use of lush *trompe-l'oeil* digital prints.

Most people experience couture clothing not through wearing the garments, but by seeing others wearing them, photographed on the runway, the red carpet, on location or in a studio.

It is the fashion photographer's role to interpret clothing and accessories, often embedding items within lavish narrative scenes. Photographer Erik Madigan Heck looks to painting, and his supersaturated pictures seem to face the past and the future simultaneously. Of his approach to shooting Katrantzou's Autumn/Winter 2011 collection 'Surreal Planes', he stated, 'I am trying to flatten the space between photography and illustration, by eliminating photographic elements and painting on different surfaces and colours in post–production, attempting to move closer towards painting itself, in process and form.'[4]

Photographer Tim Walker also refers to the art of the past in the creation of fantastical fashion images. No photographer more wholeheartedly captures the essence of Surrealism than Walker, who says, 'Surrealism is an immediate passport to our subconscious ... it articulates our dreams.'[5] He uses minimal digital intervention: everything we see was present in front of his camera, and he constantly seeks collaborators and models capable of bringing his unique vision to life. One such collaborator is actor Tilda Swinton, whom Walker first met on a pebble beach in the Scottish Highlands. Since 2011, their ambitious creative projects have taken them all over the world, from England's country gardens to the volcanic craters of Iceland and the art collections of Texas.

4 https://trendland.com/mary-katrantzou-by-erik-madigan-heck/ [accessed 7 July 2022]

5 Tim Walker, interview with Susanna Brown, 9 May 2022. Unless otherwise stated, all quotes in this essay are from Walker and are taken from the same interview with the author.

Mary Katrantzou (back), Ready-to-Wear Autumn/Winter 2011

The Surrealists' visual language has resonated with Walker since childhood:

> In my youth their work spoke very deeply to me, and I didn't really understand why. ... On an instinctive, daydreaming level, I felt very comfortable with the Surrealists. I felt very at home amongst them, and I understood the emotion of every Surrealist painting or object I encountered. [6]

The movement likewise inspired Swinton:

> Surrealism is liberating, I think, especially if you discover [it] in your early teens, as I did too, it's the perfect moment because it's about freedom. Your own unconscious is validated, and as a nascent artist it's two thumbs up to the power of your imagination as a valid vehicle to place all your faith in ...[7]

Of their work together, Swinton explains: 'Our mode of collaborating is very light and very joyful, not heavy. It feels like we're constantly walking with ghosts.'[8]

In 2012, they travelled to Las Pozas, the group of forty Surreal structures of enormous proportions nestled among pools and waterfalls in the remote subtropical rainforest of the Sierra Madre mountains, several hundred miles north of Mexico City. Built between 1949 and 1984 near the small town of Xilitla, Las Pozas is the creation of the visionary Edward James, art patron extraordinaire and champion of the Surrealist movement, whom Dali once described as 'an immensely rich English poet'.[9] James' friend George Melly called him 'the last of the great eccentrics'.[10] James died in 1984, his quixotic project unfinished, but his spirit is very much alive in the series of photographs and short film, *Stranger than Paradise*, that Walker and Swinton made in the jungle. The seed of the idea was planted by art director Jerry Stafford, a long-time admirer of Edward James, who suggested that they visit Las Pozas to photograph Swinton for *W* magazine. Walker began by delving deeply into James' life and art collection, collating a huge number of visual references, particularly works by female Surrealists including Leonora Carrington

6 Susanna Brown and Tim Walker (eds), *Tim Walker: Wonderful Things* (London: V&A, 2019), 153.

7 Ibid.

8 Ibid.

9 *The Secret Life of Edward James*, ITV, 1978, www.youtube.com/watch?v=Ooos-dgHLTGY [Accessed 10 May 2022].

10 Ibid.

107

and Remedios Varo, both of whom left Europe for Mexico and became close friends.

Dali introduced James to fellow Surrealist René Magritte, and the Belgian artist spent several months in 1937 at James' London home, painting pictures for the drawing room. Magritte's *Rêverie de Monsieur James (Mr James's Daydream)* particularly sparked Walker's curiosity. Painted in oils in 1943, it depicts seven pink roses and seven elegant hands sprouting from a single plant against an azure sky. Inspired by a dream that James recounted to the painter, it is one of the few works by Magritte with a literal title. In 1949, Magritte sent James a postcard of the finished painting and wrote, 'I painted this picture during the Occupation in memory of the happier times when I met you. You probably remember that it was you who suggested the subject of this picture?'[11]

11 David Sylvester and Sarah Whitfield (eds), *René Magritte: Catalogue raisonné, vol. II* (London: Wittenborn Art Books, 1993), 306.

The circuitous journey that took James from England to his personal Xanadu in the Mexican jungle began in the late 1930s. He travelled to New York to manage Dali's Dream of Venus — a wild Surrealist funhouse at the New York World's Fair of 1939 — then on to New Mexico and Hollywood for a period of pious introspection. He moved south to explore Mexico, 'the Surrealist place par excellence', and found Xilitla

René Magritte, *Rêverie de Monsieur James (Mr James' Daydream)*, 1943

Tilda Swinton, *Mr James's Daydream*,
Las Pozas, Mexico, 2012.
Photograph by Tim Walker

in 1945.[12] James built a small house there and, with the assistance of Plutarco Gastélum, collected tens of thousands of orchids and a menagerie of wild animals. After a freak snowfall destroyed many of his plants in 1962, he began to build a garden of poetic and whimsical concrete structures that could withstand any weather. Over many years and at a cost of some $5 million, a team of local craftsmen built dozens of Piranesi-like monuments based on James' sketches.

The House with a Roof like a Whale, the Road of the Seven Deadly Sins, the House with Three Storeys that Could be Five — the names of James' follies convey the deeply idiosyncratic nature of his project. There is a 'library' with no books and a 'cinema' with no screening room. The Stairway to Heaven is perhaps the most dramatic of all the structures. Two immense columns imitate the reproductive aspects of orchids, with two staircases coiling around them 'like skewed vertebrae'.[13] Walker photographed Swinton as a Surreal phantasm swathed in trailing fabrics, gliding up the stairway. The meticulous composition and her confident stride belie the very real danger involved in the staging of the photograph: the narrow staircase floats twenty metres above the ground without a handrail — one misstep would have spelled disaster. Swinton is reminiscent of the darkly cloaked figure ascending a staircase in Carrington's painting *The House Opposite* (1945), a whimsical work from James' collection in which rooms populated by women and girls are linked by stairs, ladders and arched doorways. The photograph also calls to mind Varo's *Arquitectura Vegetal* (*Plant Architecture*, 1962), in which cloaked figures navigate precariously narrow steps and walkways between columns resembling leafless tree trunks.

Carrington and Varo shared an interest in alchemy, astrology and witchcraft, and in Walker's pictures Swinton often appears as a witch from their paintings. Dresses by Acne Studios, Maison Margiela, Rick Owens and Rochas echo the

12 André Breton, quoted in Christopher Turner, 'The eccentric English socialite who embraced Surrealism', *Apollo* (April 2021), www.apollo-magazine.com/edward-james-surrealism-patron-salvador-dali/ [Accessed 10 May 2022].

13 Mathew Holmes, 'A Garden of Earthly Delights', *AA Files*, 66 (2013), 37.

forms of the voluminous garments worn by the mysterious characters in Carrington's *The Pomps of the Subsoil* or *The Old Maids* (both 1947). Walker describes the female Surrealists as being 'really good fashion designers and hair stylists'; gesturing to the figure whose hair forms a glowing swirl of light in Varo's *La Llamada* (*The Call*, 1961), he says, 'look at the chic little moon in her amazing orange hair'. Swinton's hair was styled by Julien d'Ys, a frequent collaborator whom Walker views as 'a contemporary Surrealist'. In several photographs, Swinton's hair streams upwards, defying gravity and evoking Dorothea Tanning's *Eine Kleine Nachtmusik* (1943), one of Walker's favourite paintings.

In other photographs, Swinton assumes the role of James himself, in a dark suit and white gloves, or appears as a continuation of the surreal environment, posing statically in front of a relief by Carrington and wearing a chequerboard-print Louis Vuitton dress and Emilio Cavallini tights to match the floor tiles. The colour palette of the shoot ranges from the lightest pastel hues to deep jewel colours, suggesting the passage of time from dawn to dusk. As twilight fell, Swinton donned a floor-sweeping Katrantzou gown in the same emerald-green as the jungle foliage: 'We suddenly found these massive leaves and we were in *Alice in Wonderland*. Our sense of scale just went insane!'[14] In one photograph, she is framed by giant leaves as she emerges from the gloaming in a pale Gucci gown and delicate mask 'as if about to attend a Surrealist ball'. She might well be channelling the spirit of Fini, who was photographed by the likes of Horst and Jack Nisberg in her lavish costumes for Surrealist parties. Swinton's intricate mask, designed by Vicki Beamon, was based on Magritte's *Shéhérazade* of 1947.

14 Susanna Brown and Tim Walker (eds), *Tim Walker: Wonderful Things* (London: V&A, 2019), 153.

In one shot, her mouth is embellished with rose gold lips, also made by Beamon, which evoke Dalí's Ruby Lips brooch. Swinton wears Beamon's pointed golden fingertips on Cornelia James gloves in powder-blue, much the same shade as Meret Oppenheim's veined suede gloves, which lend Swinton's limbs a strangely separate quality, in keeping with the Surrealist preoccupation with disembodied limbs.

René Magritte, *Shéhérazade*, 1947

Tilda Swinton with mask, Fashion: Gucci, Vicki Beamon.
Las Pozas, Mexico, 2012. Photograph by Tim Walker

Despite his detailed research and advance planning, Walker
responds instinctively, which allows space for spontaneity
during his photoshoots. Swinton recalled an extraordinary
moment of serendipity: 'My face was covered with a veil and
we found some caterpillars and decided to make eyebrows
and a moustache out of these caterpillars. I mean, I really
do feel Edward James and all the rest of the Surrealists were
cheering us on at that moment ... [It was] moving make-
up!'[15] Years later, Walker remembered, 'They had such a
pretty smell ... almonds and marzipan.'[16] Butterflies featured,
too, chiming with the Surrealists' fascination for physical
metamorphosis. James claimed he always retained a child-
like frame of mind and, like Carrington, he avoided excessive
intellectualising of art. We should perhaps approach
Walker's pictures with a similar, child-like sense of wonder,
revelling in their surreal flamboyance and magic. ▬▬▬

15 Ibid., 153.

16 Ibid., 154.

Tilda Swinton, Fashion: Giorgio Armani, Prada. Las Pozas, Mexico, 2013. Photograph by Tim Walker

above Wallis Simpson wearing Lobster dress by Elsa Schiaparelli and Salvador Dalí, c.1930s
right Cecil Beaton, Models reading in a surrealistic setting for *Vogue*, September 1936

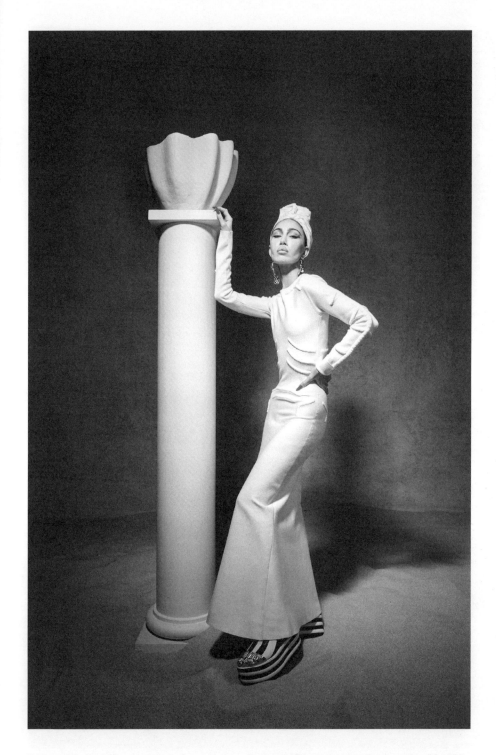

Schiaparelli by Daniel Roseberry, Long dress with three-dimensional Bone embroidery, Ready-to-Wear SS 2022

Elsa Schiaparelli designed the original, black Skeleton Dress in collaboration with Salvador Dalí in 1938. Its chunky, quilted 'bone' structure deliberately challenged conventional standards of beauty. Beyond its shock value, which both Dalí and Schiaparelli enjoyed, the dress continued the Surrealist project of making hidden realities visible. Skeleton detailing is now a signature feature of Maison Schiaparelli.

Schiaparelli by Daniel Roseberry, Shocking pink mini dress moulded from a custom sculpture and fully embroidered with glass tubes drawing a *trompe l'oeil* pattern of 'muscles', Haute Couture SS 2021

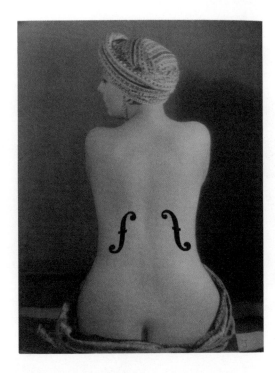

top left Man Ray, *Marcel Duchamp as Rrose Sélavy*, c.1920-1
bottom left Man Ray, *Le Violon d'Ingres (The Violin of Ingres)*, 1924
above Man Ray, France, 1937. Model wearing a Madeleine Vionnet gown in the *Brouette (Wheelbarrow)* by Óscar Domínguez

above Fashion model with painting by Man Ray, *Observatory Times: The Lovers*, 1936
right Man Ray, July 1925, France. Cover photograph for *La Révolution surréaliste* no. 4

Dora Maar, *Untitled (Hand with Shell)*, 1934

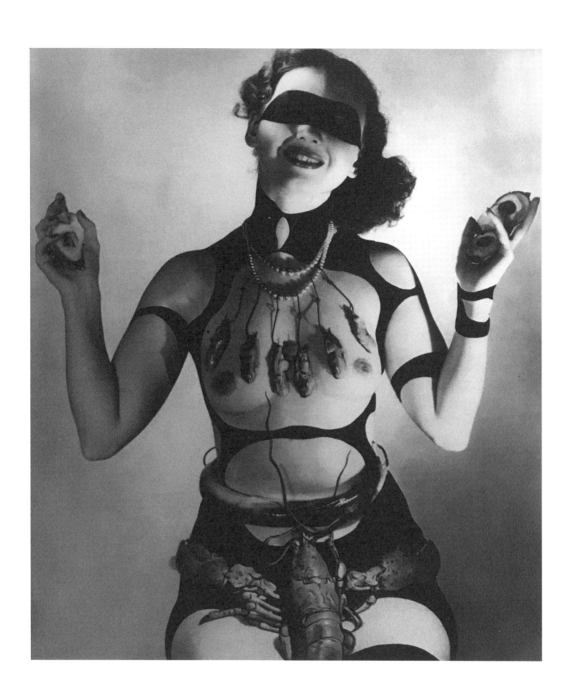

Horst P. Horst, *Costume for Salvador Dalí's Dream of Venus*, 1939

Claude Cahun, *Self-portrait (in the mirror)*, c.1928

Photographer and writer Claude Cahun troubles gender boundaries in a striking series of self-portraits. Through this medium, Cahun exploits the apparent objectivity of the camera in order to give staged performances the texture of reality.

Claude Cahun, *Self-portrait (I am in training, don't kiss me)*, c.1927

above Dora Maar, *Mannequin en maillot de bain (Model in Swimsuit)*, 1936
right Lee Miller, Bathing feature for *Vogue*, London, England, 1941

Royal Whitaker wearing Salvador Dalí's Telephone Ear Clips, 1941

above Peggy Guggenheim wearing earrings designed by Yves Tanguy, c.1950
below Peggy Guggenheim wearing earrings designed by Alexander Calder, c.1950

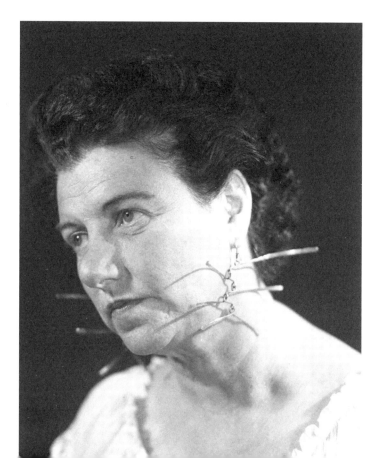

above Madelle Hegeler wearing jewellery designed by Salvador Dalí, 1959
right Philippe Halsman, *Salvador Dalí with the jewel The Eye of Time*, c.1956

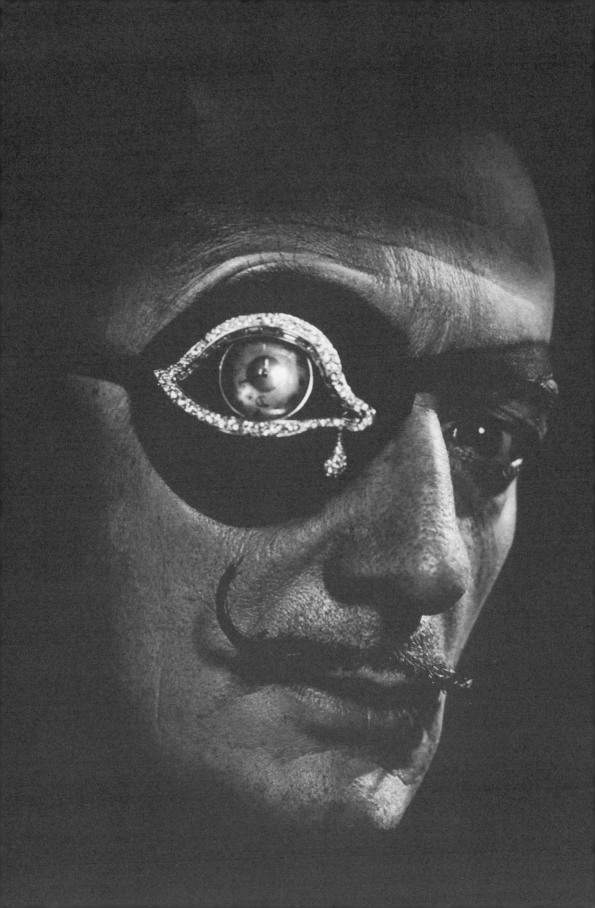

left Mary Katrantzou, Typewriter silk dress, Ready-to-Wear AW 2012

This dress transforms the body into a wearable typewriter. It recalls *trompe l'oeil* effects in Surrealist artworks, which 'trick the eye' into seeing a three-dimensional image. It also brings to mind ready-made sculptures such as Conroy Maddox's *Onanistic Typewriter I*. The digitally painted print was inspired by a vintage typewriter photographed by collector Adwoa Bagalini.

right Christian Dior by Maria Grazia Chiuri, Salvador Dalí ensemble, Haute Couture SS 2018

The design of this skirt references costumes created by Dalí and Christian Dior for a spectacular Venetian costume ball. This extravagant event was organised in 1951, at Palazzo Labia, by the fabulously wealthy and eccentric art patron Carlos de Beistegui. The jacket, meanwhile, nods to the American 'cowboy' jackets that Dalí chose to wear after his return to Europe from the United States in the 1950s and 60s.

Viviane Sassen was interviewed by
Susanna Brown, photography curator
and author. Sassen is a Dutch fashion
and fine art photographer who lives and
works in Amsterdam. She collaborates
with designers, models and musicians,
and her career encompasses a broad
array of projects, from creating an
installation at the Palace of Versailles to
directing a music video for the musician
M.I.A. and shooting editorial fashion
spreads for major magazines. Sassen's
award-winning photography has been
widely published and has been the
subject of solo exhibitions since 2001.

VIVIANE
SASSEN

&

SUSANNA
BROWN

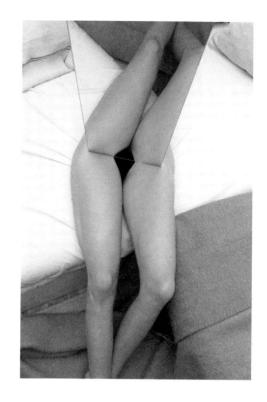

SB Thank you, Viviane, for joining me today to discuss your work in the context of Surrealism. We're going to begin with your photograph *Marte #02* from your 2014 project *Umbra*, which featured in the exhibition *Objects of Desire* [which opened at the Vitra Design Museum, Weil am Rhein, in 2019]. For this image, you used a large mirror to reflect the model's bare legs and obscure her body. The picture makes me think of the Hans Bellmer doll of 1935, which is constructed entirely from legs. Could you tell me a little more about this specific image and the inspiration for it?

Viviane Sassen, *Marte #02*, 2014

VS I know the Bellmer doll with the four legs, and the Surrealists have always been my largest source of inspiration. The way I work is very intuitive and I've always been interested in mirrors. Even as a child, I was playing games about looking: for example, covering one eye and then the other, creating these subtle shifts in your viewpoint and slightly different angles. I was also intrigued by my own reflection in the mirror. It wasn't about vanity, but looking in the way a photographer looks and making new shapes with the body. When I was very young, I would stand in front of the mirror almost naked and do weird things with my limbs, making strange shapes, and making the body deformed or different in the mirror, and that really interested me visually.

SB That's a huge theme throughout Surrealism: fragmenting the female form and playing with separate parts of the body, as well as intentionally creating something distorted, disturbing even.

VS Exactly! And looking at the whole of art history, Surrealism is the period I relate to the most. Photographers such as Claude Cahun and Man Ray, and painters like Magritte, have a great influence on me. I've always been drawn to their work. The Surrealists were part of my world from an early age, in a visual rather than an academic sense. I feel particularly connected to their use of mirrors, shadows, ideas about the body, and the playful concept of the *cadavre exquis*, which connects with what I'm doing now with collages. I'm also fascinated by the writings of the Surrealists, how they relate to the dreamworld and the subconscious.

SB Many of the early works included in the exhibition are in your mental library of images, aren't they? As we just said, the female form, both naked and clothed, is a recurring subject for Surrealists, and I'm curious to know if your own experience as a model influences your photography?

VS I think so. When I started out as a model, I was often intimidated by this 'male gaze', and I was still very young and probably didn't know how to handle it. Picking up the camera and putting myself in control of the image, and in control of my own image by making self-portraits, has been helpful for me. I can articulate a different kind of sexuality or female form in my work without the male gaze ... it can still be erotic or sensual, but it's a very different feeling when you own it yourself. Reclaiming this image of yourself is an act of feminism in a way. When I was modelling, I never had bad experiences with male photographers, but still I felt there were lingering, preconceived ideas about femininity, and an underlying misogyny in terms of the commodification of women and their bodies.

SB Staying with that subject of the erotic and the sensual, the exhibition's title was *Objects of Desire*. I'm simplifying here, but we could say that the whole fashion industry is built on the concept of desire. Is desire a major theme in your work?

VS Yes — not necessarily a sexual or erotic desire, but there is a desire for beauty and aesthetics in my work. In my pictures, I always try to capture something that's hidden, not give everything away, and that's often where the desire lies. I'm drawn to things that are beautiful but that can't be fully grasped. In a sense, photography itself is like that because it's a world somewhere else ... it's just a piece of paper or an image, but the viewer has a desire to step into the world that's depicted in the photographs. That connects to the idea of the mirror, longing to be on the other side of the mirror, to enter that parallel world; I'm interested in parallel universes. I think unfulfilled desire is beautiful, sometimes even more so than when it's fulfilled.

SB Your pictures can be tantalising in that way: we see glimpses of things but not the whole story, and the atmosphere of mystery and strangeness in your work is very powerful. It leads us to ask: Why?

vs It's about humour, too. If it's only beauty in darkness, it might become tacky — but with Surrealism, there's often humour there. It seems like those early artists also had the ability to laugh about themselves or mock themselves, and I can relate to that.

sb It's important not to take yourself too seriously ...

vs At the same time, it's been important for me to be able to take this tool of power, the camera, and collaborate with other women. Sometimes I work only with women, and I find those projects can be very empowering and freeing. I created two books with my muse Roxane, which are about the power of femininity. I really like the idea of femininity that can be aggressive or subversive, even ugly, and I think a lot about these boundaries. As women, we don't always have to be docile, neat or pretty.

sb Absolutely. It's so important as a woman to recognise and take control of your own power. I'd like to move on to something you've spoken about in the past: the subject of dreams.

vs From a very young age, I thought that my dream life, the hours I was asleep, were equally as important as my waking life. It comes back to the idea of parallel universes. In the daytime, I would soak up all the impressions from everything around me, but at night I would do the same thing in my dreams. The dream world is so connected to the subconscious and Surrealism. My own dreams are often really clear, and can be an important source of inspiration. When I was working in Africa, I had very vivid dreams and I would wake up with these strong images in my head. I'd make small drawings based on those mental images and set out to realise them in my photographs.

SB That makes me think of Salvador Dali, who believed that the state between wakefulness and sleep was the most creative for the brain and considered dreams central to his process. And Dali believed that Surrealist objects – those playful yet menacing objects made from the conjunction of items not normally associated – could reveal the secret desires of the unconscious. I think that brings us back to the subject of your collages. Where do you source images, and do you plan them in advance in your head?

VS No, not at all, but since childhood I have loved making collages. During the Covid-19 pandemic, obviously I couldn't travel much, which has always been the best way for me to work. So, instead, I began to dig into my archive. I have so many prints, and I just started cutting them up and creating new shapes. Before Covid, I did a collage project called *Of Mud and Lotus*, and right now I'm also working on collages.

Viviane Sassen, *Consequences / Cadavre Exquis #2*, 2020

SB Interestingly, you use your previous work for the collages rather than found images, which is quite different from how the early Surrealists worked.

VS That's right, I only use my own photographs. I begin by making them quite small, but if I want to enlarge them later it can be like looking for a needle in a haystack. For example, I'll look at a leg or a hand in the small collage and ask myself, 'Where did I get this, which shoot is it from?' And then I have to search through my archive for the leg, and that can be quite frustrating sometimes ...

SB I think that's quite a surreal mental image — searching for a specific leg within hundreds of legs piled together! You've worked with so many different fashion designers, from Stella McCartney to Hermès, Miu Miu and Dries Van Noten. Which contemporary designers do you think are particularly surreal in their approach?

VS Jonathan Anderson comes to mind first — you can see how he's inspired by sculpture and how he transforms elements he finds in art into clothes. The way he works with material, colour and shape is very much drawn from art, which I find very interesting. And, of course, what Martin Margiela has done in the past is also amazing.

SB Another photographer who features in this book is Tim Walker. He works in a highly collaborative way with hair and make-up artists, stylists, set designers and so on, and he's been working closely with some of the same people for more than twenty years. Surrealist artists often worked in collaboration with photographers too: I'm especially thinking of the projects that

Viviane Sassen, *Roxane II*, 2017

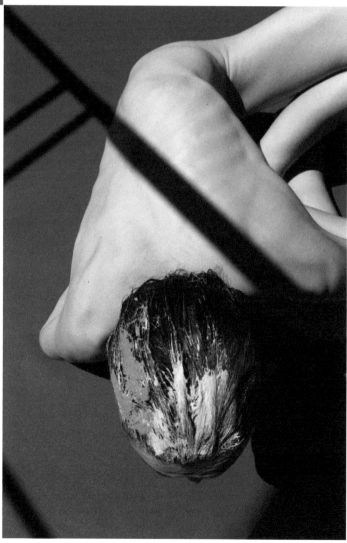

Dali and Horst P. Horst did together in the 1930s. You also collaborate with big teams, but sometimes you work alone on your art projects. Can we talk more about these two different approaches ... which do you prefer?

vs I often say my art and my fashion work are two different sides of my personality. The art is a much more solitary process, and I enjoy that, but I really love collaborations — and in fashion it's always about that. Other creative people bring so much to the table that I can't bring. I tend to collaborate with women more than men, and I also enjoy collaborating with writers to complement my pictures. There are certain models that I've been photographing for years, and that's very special — we've built these bonds of faith which enable us to explore new things and be incredibly daring ... you need to know someone for a while before you're able to do that.

sb When I watch fashion photographers working, I'm fascinated by the silent gestural communication that can happen between the photographer and their favourite models.

vs It's like a silent dance. I'm quite shy, so I can't have that level of intimacy with everyone. But when it happens, you both get into this zone of creating things without fear. It's an amazing feeling when you let the fear go, and you're both riding the wave together — you come into a flow of creativity. Sometimes it's with a model, but I've also experienced it a lot with the stylist Vanessa Reid. We get into the zone and into a flow where we can create things together and bounce ideas around ... we can go a little bit crazy! ▬▬▬

right Viviane Sassen, Marte Mei van Haaster in Jonathan Anderson, 2019

Sarah Lucas, *Cigarette Tits [Idealized Smokers Chest II]*, 1999

TAKE YOUR DESIRES FOR REALITY: SURREALISM & THE OBJECT

WHAT I HAVE WANTED TO DO ABOVE ALL IS TO SHOW THE PRECAUTIONS AND THE RUSES, WHICH DESIRE, IN SEARCH OF ITS OBJECT, EMPLOYS AS IT WAVERS IN PRECONSCIOUS WATERS, AND ONCE THIS OBJECT IS DISCOVERED, THE MEANS IT USES TO REVEAL IT THROUGH CONSCIOUSNESS.
ANDRÉ BRETON [1]

Man Ray, *Slipper Spoon*, 1934. For André Breton's *L'Amour fou*, 1937

1 André Breton, *Mad Love* (1937), trans. Mary Ann Caws (Lincoln: University of Nebraska Press, 1987), 24-5.

2 Alyce Mahon, *Surrealism and the Politics of Eros, 1938-1968* (London: Thames & Hudson, 2005), 15.

3 André Breton, 'First Surrealist Manifesto' (1924), in *Manifestoes of Surrealism*, trans. Richard Seaver and Helen R. Lane (Ann Arbor: University of Michigan Press, 1969), 3 and 9.

The concept of the object and the concept of desire were equally important to the Surrealist movement. The ambition to marry the inanimate with the animate ran through its every endeavour, reflecting its commitment to transform the world through Eros, the life drive.[2] As André Breton asserted in the first Surrealist manifesto of 1924, man was an 'inveterate dreamer' but incarcerated by 'the reign of logic' enforced by civilisation and progress.[3] His chains had to be broken, his mind and its desires and fears set free. The object could be a sensate or inert thing; it could be purchased, imagined, discovered in a dream or in a person, but the element of desire was central to its creative potential, ensuring the dynamic between the material and the immaterial was made tangible.

Breton's *Nadja* (1928) exemplifies early Surrealist explorations of objecthood and desire in the name of self-discovery. The semi-autobiographical novel centres on the numerous objects Breton encounters in Paris, including an enigmatic young woman named Nadja. He gets in touch with his unconscious by his touching of 'things', whether a lover or a new book. In Breton's later novel *Mad Love* (1937), this strategy of rerouting the everyday object to open up desire continues. Visiting the Saint-Ouen flea market, Breton finds and purchases a curious 'wooden spoon ... of peasant fabrication but quite beautiful' with a little shoe in the handle. This leads him to pontificate on Cinderella and his sexual longing for a new woman. Breton does not cite Sigmund Freud – for whom a concave vessel like a shoe typically signifies the female, while an intruding object like a spoon connotes the male – but advises the reader that the simplest, unusual object can 'reveal' desire if 'preconscious waters' are explored.[4]

4 André Breton, *Nadja* (New York: Grove Press, 1928), 60.

In 1929, the German cultural critic Walter Benjamin wrote approvingly of the transformational, object-oriented aesthetics in Surrealism, noting,

> No one before these visionaries and augurs perceived how destitution – not only social but architectonic, the poverty of interiors, enslaved and enslaving objects – can suddenly be transformed into revolutionary nihilism.[5]

5 Walter Benjamin, 'Surrealism, The Last Snapshot of the European Intelligentsia', in *One Way Street and Other Writings*, trans. Edmund Jephcott, Kingsley Shorter (London: Verso, 1979), 229.

Benjamin recognised that the Surrealist strategy of *détournement* (hijacking) of the designed object not only opened up 'the vividness and richness of associations which [the object] arouses', but could also liberate society from consumerism and totalitarianism. Surrealism represented a critical intellectual force against fascism, which was steadily gaining ground across Europe.[6]

6 Ibid., 146.

In a 1934 lecture, 'Qu'est-ce que le Surréalisme?' ('What is Surrealism?'), Breton explained that the Surrealists would focus on the object to 'aid the systematic derangement of all the senses'.[7] Freud's writings were seminal to their understanding of how a banal object could take on such sensory potential. In *Three Essays on the Theory of Sexuality* (1905), translated into French in 1926, Freud explained how the desired object could reveal three main desiring trajectories: heterosexual (a desire for the opposite sex), homosexual (a desire for the same sex) or voyeurism (a desire to look). He also argued that every finding of the object of desire was actually 'a re-finding of it' as our first desire and erotic pleasure begins at the mother's breast.[8] Thus objects of desire are not 'things', but creative processes, often leading us back to a repressed fantasy, fetish or pleasure.

7 André Breton, 'Surrealist Situation of the Object' in *Manifestoes of Surrealism*, 263.

8 Sigmund Freud, 'Three Essays on the Theory of Sexuality' (1905) in *The Standard Edition of the Complete Psychological Works of Sigmund Freud*, Volume 7 (1901-1905), ed., James Strachey (London: Hogarth Press, 1953), 222

If Breton called for a focus on the object, then women Surrealists led the way in producing them for the collective, and as a means to refashion the dominant image of woman as object of desire par excellence. Meret Oppenheim's animalistic *Object/Luncheon in Fur* (1936) and Claude Cahun's *Object* (1936), with its quizzical eyeball, paved the way, but this essay will concentrate on the objects designed by Argentinian-born Leonor Fini, Canadian Mimi Parent and the American Dorothea Tanning. These artists' exploration of the Janus-faced potential of the object to derail the male gaze as well as the socio-political status quo played a critical role in the Surrealist movement's impact on high and low culture alike, as well as its legacy in the work of contemporary women artists.

Leonor Fini's *Corset Chair* (1939) brings together two recognisable objects, beautifully elucidating the dynamics

Leonor Fini, design for Elsa Schiaparelli perfume 'Shocking', 1937

of desire expressed in fashion and furniture, but with a Surrealist twist. First exhibited at 17 Place Vendome in Paris, right beside Elsa Schiaparelli's haute couture salon, the chair resembles a corset, its stripes of ebony and mother-of-pearl topped with a black bow, belying its metal form and daring the viewer to untie it. Fini's design for Schiaparelli's perfume 'Shocking' also revelled in the idea of the female knowingly displaying her sexual prowess through a self-fashioning. The glass bottle was modelled on the hourglass figure of Hollywood siren Mae West, the details of a floral lid and tailor's measuring tape ensuring the smell and touch of a woman were explicitly invoked.

Just as Dali's contemporary homage to Mae West in the voluptuous red Mae West Lips sofa (1937) explored the film star's femme fatale image, so Fini's design exaggerated the power of the feminine masquerade to entrap and seduce.

The Surrealists' critique of consumerism and authoritarianism continued, and took on new forms, during the Cold War. In their 1959 collective exhibition titled *EROS* (*Exposition inteRnatiOnale du Surréalisme*), the Surrealists took the sensorial assault on the object even further in asking the public to enter the Daniel Cordier Gallery in Paris through a vulvic-shaped beaded glass door. This metaphoric rebirth was greeted with the smell of a floral perfume that was sprayed from small pipes in the walls, which in turn appeared to sigh orgasmically thanks to a sound piece by Radovan Ivšić.[9] As one critic observed, the public was put in the role of 'a voyeur [rather] than a viewer'.[10] And yet the Surrealists were not pandering to traditional, male voyeurism, as the poster for the *EROS* exhibition made clear by featuring one particular object from the show — Mimi Parent's *Masculine-*

9 Mahon,*Surrealism and the Politics of Eros*, 159.

10 Pierre Schneider, 'Art News from Paris', *Art News*, 58 (February 1960), 44.

Poster for *Exposition Internationale du Surréalisme*,
Galerie Daniel Cordier, Paris, 1959

Feminine (1959): a (masculine) tie made from her own (feminine) hair.

Parent's object signalled how traditional, poetic and painterly explorations of desire that often luxuriated in the connotations of unbound female hair could be turned on their head. In her work, fantasies and fears of the castrated, hairy female sex or a fetishism for cross-dressing could be happily explored (cross-dressing was enjoyed by many in the Surrealist circle, including Claude Cahun and Toyen). *Masculine-Feminine* serves as the perfect Surrealist prop in its defiance of binarism. The fact that Parent's work was chosen for the poster reinforces the wider Surrealist group's commitment to promoting women artists and to dismantling the traditional institutions of power that policed woman and desire alike – notably the Family, Church and State.

Dorothea Tanning also employed the handmade object to explore new avenues for fetishism. *Pincushion to Serve as Fetish* (1965) was made from banal domestic materials: black velvet, white paint, an oil funnel and sewing pins that punctured the velvet haphazardly. The object's crudely fashioned form stood in opposition to the mass-produced consumer product and the vogue for hard-edge, minimalist sculpture in the 1960s. It also invited psychic responses and play – Tanning described it as 'bristling with images'.[11]

11 Dorothea Tanning,
Birthday and Beyond,
(Philadelphia:
Philadelphia Museum,
2001), np.

As an archetypal domestic object, the pincushion invoked the problem of the 'feminine mystique' identified by feminist activist Betty Friedan in 1963. In her study, Friedan wrote of the American media's promotion of 'the home sewing industry' as an acceptable vehicle of feminine

12 Betty Friedan, *The Feminine Mystique* (1963), (Middlesex: Penguin Books, 1965), 196.

creativity, an activity that was perceived as allowing the wife and mother to 'realise their own individuality' but within the safety of the home.[12] Equally, Tanning's choice of black velvet mocks the maternal lack of which Freud wrote in his reading of the male fetishist's penchant for hair, fur and velvet, while the detail of a little paw-like stump to the side of the object signalled the power of the liberated imagination to animate the inanimate. Desire was also explored through the object's materiality and the choice, feel and experience of the cloth – the dark velvet's sensuality emphasised by the white vein-like lines of paint that decorate it. Tanning willed her materials to elicit desire:

> I've always been excited by a piece of woven cloth ... Something ancient and sensuous rises in me to greet and touch and manipulate this first of man's refinements – first of his inventions not devoted to survival.[13]

13 Dorothea Tanning in Monique Levi-Strauss, 'Dorothea Tanning: Soft Sculptures', *American Fabrics and Fashions*, 108 (Fall 1976), 68-69.

Pincushion to Serve as Fetish offered new beginnings, as materiality leads to a desiring process.

Surrealism's 'ridiculing and reshuffling' of commodity culture through the quasi-ethnographic strategy of stripping objects of their intended function and investing them with a new symbolic and erotic function challenged the system of desire and consumption on which the modern economy operates. Unsurprisingly, it has inspired legacies in feminist art globally in recent times.[14] The YBA artist Sarah Lucas beautifully teases out the continued flattering of the male eye as well as the persistence of Freudian ideas in contemporary culture in *Cigarette Tits [Idealized Smokers Chest II]* (1999). Lucas' use of the cigarette to form bulbous breasts suspended in a black bra hung on a schoolroom chair cleverly references Freud's now famous reading of infantile sexuality and the first oral stage – which evidences a libidinous, 'cannibalistic' sexual organisation – as well as his reading of the cigarette (or pencil) as a nipple substitute.[15] Lucas' use of cigarettes for the work may also be read as a 'laddish' subversion of wider cultural references

14 James Clifford, *The Predicament of Culture: Twentieth-Century Ethnography, Literature, and Art* (Cambridge MA: Harvard University Press, 1988), 121 and 551.

15 Freud, 'Three Essays on the Theory of Sexuality', 198.

16 Martin Maloney, 'Everyone a Winner! Selected British Art from the Saatchi Collection 1987-97' in Norman Rosenthal et al., *Sensation* (London: Royal Academy of Arts, 1997), 3.

to cigarettes and their promise of pleasure despite their threat to one's health. One thinks of the 'Marlboro Man' who gave a rugged cowboy face to the Philip Morris tobacco brand between 1954 and 1999, and the appropriation of that mass-marketed masculinity by the Pictures Generation artist Richard Prince in his *Untitled (Cowboy)* series of the 1980s. Lucas reprises these sexual and cultural references, and the myth of masculinity that underpinned them. At the same time, her act of hijacking employs a tongue-in-cheek humour – she has often staged self-portraits in which she smokes with mannish flair, as in *Smoking* (1998).[16]

17 Nina Saunders in Pennina Barnett, 'Purity and Fear', *MAKE: The Magazine of Women's Art,* Issue 74, (February-March 1997).

As a Danish-born artist who trained at Central Saint Martins College of Art and Design in London, Nina Saunders offers what might be described as an outsider's view of British culture: taking familiar pieces of furniture and fashioning them into strange new beasts that bristle with suggestion, much like Tanning's sculptures. Saunders described her large white sculpture *Pure Thought IV* (1997), a white sphere ten feet in diameter, as 'something that could contain hidden things, growing and bursting'.[17] On the one hand, this object is familiar due to its chesterfield sofa-like leatherette material and buttoning. On the other hand, it is unfamiliar in its gargantuan breast-like form, looming large over the viewer's space. The artist invokes the power of class and wealth in referencing the chesterfield while simultaneously using scale and texture to mock Freud's conception of the uncanny as often triggered by the return of a repressed desire. *The Whirlwind is in the Thorn Bush: Conquest* (2017) continues this play as a period sofa appears to birth a bulbous bodily form. The work perfectly extends the Surrealists' intrigue with anthropomorphism and seems to pay homage to Tanning's soft sculptural installation *Hôtel du Pavot: Chambre 202* (1970-3) in which walls, chairs, a sofa and a table all sprout erotically soft limbs, arched bellies and fingers. As with Tanning's nightmarish interior, the frisson of Saunders' *Conquest* relies on a Surrealist sense of metamorphosis as the spectator witnesses the 'civilised' turning bestial.[18]

18 See Alyce Mahon, 'Daughters of the Minotaur: Women Surrealists' Re-Enchantment of the World', in Cecilia Alemani, *The Milk of Dreams*, 59th Venice Biennale, (Venice: Silvana Editoriale, 2022), 88-93.

Najla El Zein, *Stroke*, *Sensorial Brushes* series, 2014

Lebanese designer Najla El Zein's description of her practice also echoes the aesthetic of Surrealism: 'Design has been a way for me to dissect and analyse every emotion, every thought, every impression, putting a form to it, test it, touch it, get closer to it.'[19] El Zein emphasises the psychic and erotic power of tenderness and touch through the use of surprisingly hard, cold materials. In her series of paired objects titled *Seduction*, abstracted marble shapes overlap, stand adjacent, or nestle together like spent lovers or a mother and child, their cold surfaces curiously augmenting the mood and feel of intimacy and connection.

Her series *Sensorial Brushes* continues this tactile play as prickly hay, false eyelashes and feathers sprout from smooth Pentelic marble objects. They are domestic in scale and are described by the artist as 'marble-sculpted pleasure tools' for the public.[20] Small sensory brushes are often used as an aid for adults and children with general sensory dysregulation, and here the artist makes such an object aesthetically beautiful as well as functional, while also willing everyone to touch, tickle, scratch and to indulge the senses over the rational mind. Indeed, these brushes revel in an idea much favoured by the Surrealists, expressed by the verb *frôler* — to brush against.[21] The legacy of the Surrealist object and the avant-garde approach to design lies in this haptic richness and its individual and collective potential — for art to touch us and open up new desires and connections, without fear of the consequences. ▬▬

19 Najla El Zein, artist entry, Friedman Benda Gallery, New York, www.friedmanbenda. com/artists/najla-elzein [accessed 27 July 2022].

20 Dan Howarth, 'Sensorial Brushes by Najla El Zein', *Dezeen*, (18 December 2014), www.dezeen. com/2014/12/18/ sensorial-brushes-najla-el-zein-workspace-pleasure-tools-stimulate-the-skin [accessed 27 July 2022].

21 See Julia Kelly, 'Prière de Frôler: The Touch in Surrealism', in Jennifer Mundy (ed.), *Surrealism: Desire Unbound*, (London: Tate Publishing & NJ: Princeton, 2001), 79-85.

Dorothea Tanning, *Pincushion to Serve as Fetish*, 1979 edition of 1965 design

Lee Bul, *Untitled (Anagram Leather #8 T.O.T.)*, 2003/2018

Bul's *Anagram* sculpture and drawing series recombines interchangeable parts into new forms, just as anagrams are made by rearranging the letters of another word. These jointed, overlapping leather constructions are reminiscent of plant or insect bodies, perhaps from a futuristic universe of mutating forms. Bul's work questions existing physical norms and expectations, often with reference to literature and science fiction.

above Dorothea Tanning, *Chambre 202, Hôtel du Pavot*, 1970-3, Tate Modern, 2019
right Sarah Lucas, *Cigarette Tits [Idealized Smokers Chest II]*, 1999

Ruth Francken, *Homme*, 1971

Allen Jones, *Chair*, 1969

Not many sculptures provoke such controversy as this 'chair' in the form of a mannequin wearing bondage gear. Feminist activists in the 1970s vandalised it with paint stripper. Jones' work recalls the eroticised mannequins in the 1938 *Exposition Internationale du Surréalisme*. Both provoked shock in proportion to their power to seduce.

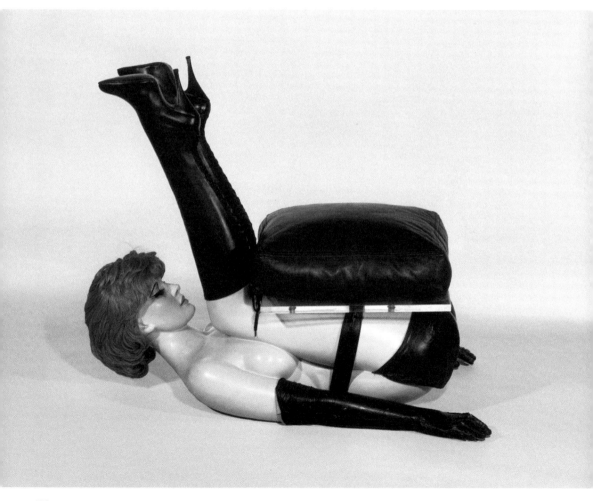

Studio Wieki Somers, *High Tea Pot*, 2003

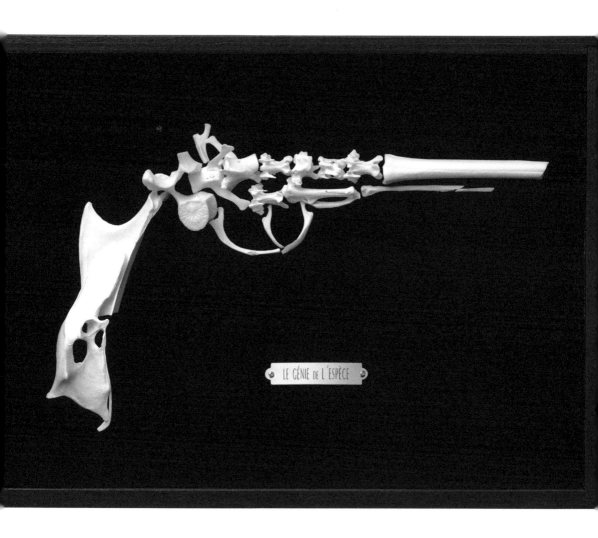

LE GÉNIE DE L'ESPÈCE

Wolfgang Paalen, *Le Génie de l'espèce (The Genius of the Species)*, 1938

This arrangement of animal bones in the shape of a revolver is an ominous symbol of past and future death. The title is a quote from philosopher Friedrich Nietzsche and his argument that human consciousness is inseparable from our need to communicate and find safety within social structures. Paalen's work, created just before the outbreak of the Second World War in 1939, highlights the tragic irony that society can also be humanity's biggest threat.

Victor Brauner, *Espace psychologique (Psychological Space)*, 1939

Victor Brauner, *Loup-Table* in *Exposition Internationale du Surréalisme*, 1947

below Kurt Seligmann, *Ultra-Meuble* in *Exposition Internationale du Surréalisme*, 1938
right Hans Bellmer, *Untitled (La Poupée/The Doll)*, c.1936

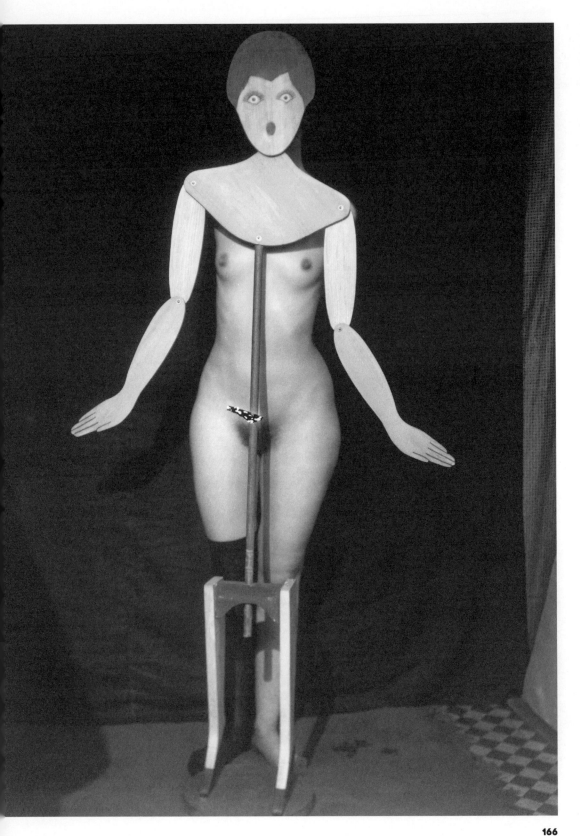

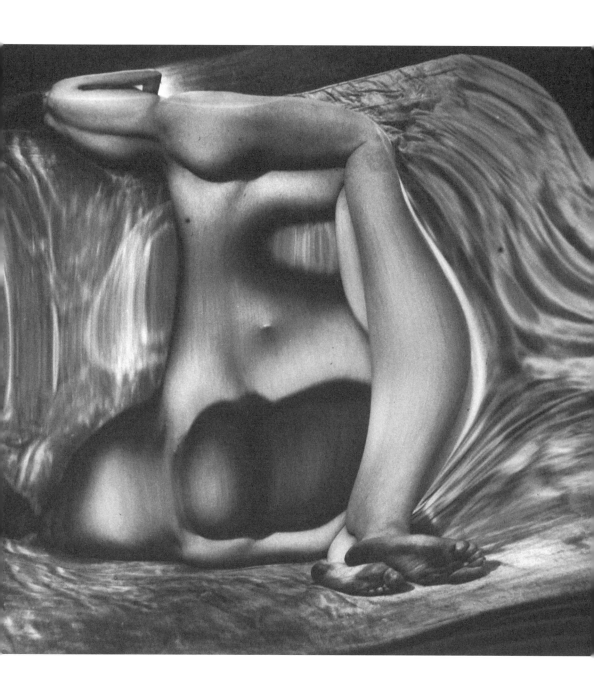

left Man Ray, *The coat-stand (Le porte-manteau)*, 1920
above André Kertész, *Distortion #135*, 1933

above Maurice Henry, *mannequin* in *Exposition Internationale du Surréalisme*, 1938

right Salvador Dalí, Venus dreaming inside the Dream of Venus, 1939

When Salvador Dalí designed the Dream of Venus Pavilion for the 1939 New York World's Fair, he envisioned a dark, womb-like environment. He rejected the bright, light, Modernist aesthetic that dominated the Fair. The entrance was set between two giant plaster legs. Inside, semi-clad female performers posed as mermaids among the trappings of Dalí's erotic fantasies, including lobsters and telephones.

following spread Meret Oppenheim, *Festin cannibal (The Cannibal Feast)*, re-enacted at *Exposition Internationale du Surréalisme*, 1959-60

In 1959, Meret Oppenheim tested ethical and aesthetic limits by restaging the 'consumption' of the female body for *Exposition inteRnatiOnale du Surréalisme* (*EROS*), a Surrealist exhibition exploring the wide-ranging subject of eroticism. The performance presented an elaborate banquet of food served on a nude mannequin body and invited participants to feast. Oppenheim had debuted the work earlier in 1959 for the Spring Festival in Bern, Switzerland. André Breton, the Surrealist movement's founding member, invited her to re-enact the work for *EROS* later that year.

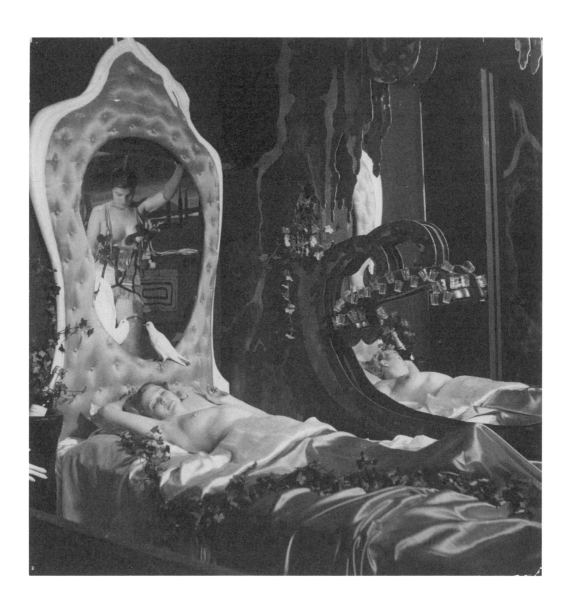

Najla El Zein was interviewed by Kathryn Johnson, Design
Museum curator of the exhibition *Objects of Desire:
Surrealism and Design 1924 – Today*. El Zein's sculptural
artworks express themes of the unconscious, sensuality and
desire. Her first solo exhibition in 2019, *Transition*, was held
at Friedman Benda, New York, and institutions such as the
Victoria and Albert Museum in London hold her work in
their permanent collections. Having graduated in product
design and interior architecture from École Camondo in Paris,
El Zein is currently based between Amsterdam and Beirut.

NAJLA
EL ZEIN

&

KATHRYN
JOHNSON

KJ Shall we start by talking about the
way you like to work? You've mentioned
that your art often gives form to personal
emotions and experiences. Would you say
your creative process is quite instinctive?

NEZ I usually start off with models. I enjoy
the spontaneous way of working with my
hands, particularly with clay, where the
gestures are intuitive and quick. Working
with my hands allows me to process certain
intuitions that I have, which are never
clear at first. It is through this process that
I am able to put my thoughts in order.
It's a form of expression where thinking
becomes a sort of manual activity. Despite
the instinctive approach, it is also a long
process, where one model leads to many
others and every step of the process is
crucial to reaching the right expression.

Najla El Zein, *Hay, Sensorial Brushes* series, 2014

KJ Your surprising choice of materials is one of the things I really enjoy about your work. It gives it a magical quality. I'm thinking of when you make marble or toothpicks look soft, for example. What informs these choices?

NEZ I do often play with the contrast between the materials and the way they are being used or formed, but that isn't always my starting point. What I wish to express through my work leads me to make conscious choices about the material. These come through a series of events, chances, moments, intuitions ...

I never really set out to transform toothpicks into fur. The toothpick just happened to have the right characteristics for me to use as if it was hair. It's also sharp, which was something I was looking for. The challenge was to make it soft and prickly at the same time in order to support the original concept I had for my project *Sitt el Sitteit* (*Lady of All Ladies*). The title is an expression in Arabic that describes a specific type of woman: powerful, inspiring, elegant and feminine. One needs to be careful in how one approaches and caresses the fur, the same way one would approach a *Sitt el Sitteit*.

The way I work with stone also supports the concept of the work. The *Seduction* series illustrates two bodies that are trying to reconcile with each other. Stone seemed to be the right material to express what it means for these bodies to embrace each other — the challenges involved. I wanted to make stone, a cold and rigid material, turn into a soft and warm material because

174

that was the original intention in the story I wanted to tell. Working with stone was a revelation to me. It is a material that is very collaborative, which leads you where you need to go. It is also a long process, and there is this unique moment while sculpting where the stone suddenly transforms and reveals itself and comes to life. It always surprises me.

KJ That's a beautiful thought. Your stone sculptures do have this incredible life and sensuality about them. I was so interested to hear that *Seduction*, and *Distortion* too, were informed by your experience of pregnancy and birth. Could you tell me a little more about the process of creating these works?

NEZ Pregnancy is a stage in life that is transformational. As a woman, a lover, a mother, an artist, I needed to juggle between all kinds of emotions. It was beautiful and scary at the same time. I am what I create — this is how I express myself and it was through my work that I was able to understand these new steps in my life, which changed me forever. It was really through making these pieces and this body of work that I was able to experience, touch, feel and embrace these changes. I needed to make them in order to understand who I was.

KJ I can relate to that. And to bring us back to the present, what are you interested in and working on at the moment?

NEZ The interactions I have and create with the people around me are very important to me, and I believe are felt in my work. My inspirations come from various places and moments, but specifically from the people I interact with: from my coworkers and my craftspeople to my friends and my family. Interactions are at the core of the project I've been working on for three years now. It is my most ambitious project, a public commission that will be revealed in October 2022 in Doha, Qatar. The permanent installation is called *Us, Her, Him* and is composed of a series of sculptural benches which span more than 313 metres of hand-sculpted stone.

The benches illustrate various modes and strata of human interactions such as acquaintances, friendships, love, introversion, confidence, familiarity, fluidity and obstruction. It was important for me to talk about human interactions for an installation that is located in the public realm. After all, that is what a public space is about — bringing people together. But also, it was important to show how much human interaction, especially in the world we live in today, is a basic need. It reminds us that collectivity is the true driving force for individual fulfilment. ▬▬▬

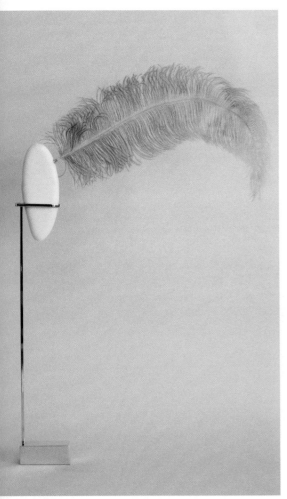

Najla El Zein, *Tickle, Sensorial Brushes* series, 2014

Najla El Zein, *Scratch, Sensorial Brushes* series, 2014

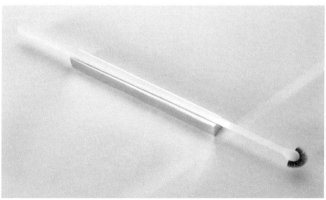

Najla El Zein, *Blink, Sensorial Brushes* series, 2014

NE
DIRE

AFRO-
REALIS
A R
AF
INTELLI

EW
ECTIONS

SUR
SM
IFICIAL
GENCE

SURREALISM
AFRO——

*Dumas' power lay in his skill at creating an
entirely different world organically connected to
this one. The stories are fables; a mythological
presence pervades. They are morality tales, magical,
resonating dream emotions and images; shifting
ambiguous terror, mystery, implied revelation. But
they are also stories of real life, now or whenever,
constructed in weirdness and poetry in which the
contemporaneity of essential themes is clear.*

Amiri Baraka, 'Henry Dumas: Afro-Surreal Expressionist',
preface to *Ark of Bones* by Henry Dumas, 1974

Afro-Surrealism, like Surrealism, has its roots in literature
and film. The writer Amiri Baraka coined the term
'Afro-Surreal' in 1974 to describe Henry Dumas' storytelling
style. In 1973, film director Djibril Diop Mambéty released
Touki Bouki, a film that brought fantasy and harsh
reality together in an unsettling blend that has since come
to define Afro-Surrealist cinema. Contemporary film-makers
including Ryan Coogler, Kahlil Joseph, Arthur Jafa,
Jenn Nkiru, Jordan Peele and Boots Riley spearheaded
the revival and popularisation of the genre in the 2010s.

Now Afro-Surrealism is a powerful force shaping the
designed world too. An exciting fusion of modern technology
with myth and psychology runs through the work of diverse
creatives: in architecture, Diébédo Francis Kéré or Kunlé
Adeyemi combine traditional building methods and
materials with high-tech engineering; in fashion, Selly Raby

Kane or Lisa Folawiyo transform customary African prints with contemporary cuts, and Yasmina Atta (interviewed here) blends references to Nigerian Hausa architecture and mythology with pop culture-inspired forms; in furniture and product design, Yinka Ilori and Atang Tshikare subvert and animate established forms with unexpected colours, materials and textures.

Despite clear resonances and resemblances, it is hard at this point to speak of 'Afro-Surrealist design' as a cohesive movement. Rather, Afro-Surrealism provides an impulse which film-makers, writers, artists and designers respond to in myriad ways. While critics draw up theoretical borders, these creatives are making work that is fluid, evolving and fantastic. ▬▬▬

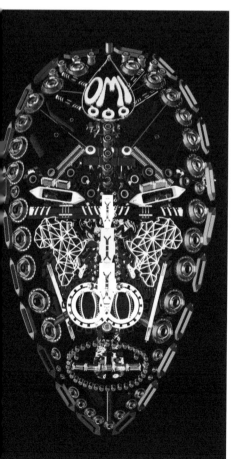

left VINCE FRASER, digital mask design inspiring the OSHUN OMI collection, 2021

This jewellery collection is inspired by Fraser's Afro-Surrealist digital art. The intricate design celebrates Oshun and Ase, mythological deities of the west-African Yoruba people. Fraser's work amplifies and uplifts Black culture while delving into spirituality, identity and ancestral history.

above Maya Deren, *A Study in Choreography for Camera*, 1945

Deren's pioneering works play with the movement of bodies in space and time, to create sequences in which reality is impossible to distinguish from dream and hallucination. Prior to becoming a film-maker, Deren worked with Katherine Dunham's dance troupe, including the dancer Talley Beatty. The film she made with Beatty exploits the power of the camera to surpass human physical limitations and endow the body with otherworldly beauty.

YASMINA ATTA

&

AYOOLA SOLARIN

Fashion designer Yasmina Atta was interviewed by Ayoola Solarin, an arts and culture writer based in London. Atta is a recent graduate in Fashion Design Womenswear from Central Saint Martins. Currently developing her practice in London, her garments and accessories draw on aspects of her Nigerian heritage blended with futuristic and mythological elements. Since Atta's graduate collection was shown in 2020, her work has been published in independent magazines, featured in a music video by the artist Celeste and displayed at galleries across London.

Yasmina Atta, Kosmos in Blue, 2020

AS When someone says 'surreal', what are the first three words that come to mind?

YA Spirit, magic and truth.

AS Your 2020 graduate collection, called Kosmos in Blue, felt like an amalgamation of your Nigerian heritage and Western culture. How do you find the balance of inspiration in your design process?

YA When I was living in Nigeria, my daily life was a combination of both Nigerian and Western influences. I feel it is always important in my work to have a balance. Even if something is playful, there might be a kind of manipulation of technique going on, or I might use a more experimental approach to materials, bend and mix things. [For Kosmos in Blue] I worked with mechanisms to make the parts move, and a lot of pieces are quite sculptural. I used heavy materials, like leather, metals, wools — quite decadent materials that I try to make move in an elegant way, which is quite strange because of their weight. I also look a lot at Nollywood films, where people mix a lot of different styles. It's quite instinctual, the way I work.

AS Along with Western and Nigerian culture, Kosmos in Blue takes inspiration from the Japanese franchise *Gundam*, which depicts transforming robots. Is transformation and evolution a running theme for you?

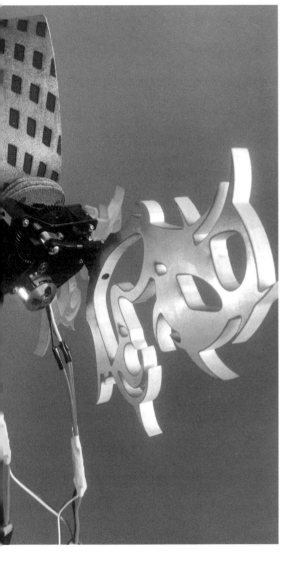

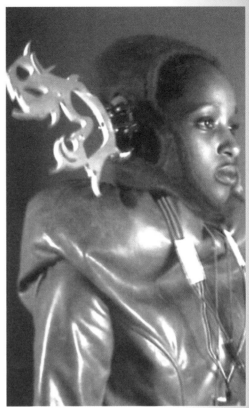

Yasmina Atta, Kosmos in Blue, 2020

YA At the moment I am looking a lot more at antique objects for inspiration, but in my personal life I do take inspiration from video-game visuals. *Gundam*, for example, is very visually appealing to me [and] the way the colour is used in a lot of anime, like *Akira*. Visually they are very exciting, and they help the way I work because I tend to lean towards old objects and combining those aspects. I like to combine things that do not make sense. I think this is the more playful side of my work which I am embracing now.

AS *Surrealism and Design Now: From Dali to AI* deals with what the movement was exploring. You mentioned Nollywood as inspiration, which is arguably peak absurdity. Can you talk a little bit about how absurdity and Surrealism play a role in your work?

YA I became interested in Surrealism because of the way the artists put an emphasis on the now. At the time I was working on Kosmos, I was looking at a lot of African cinema. They have these moments in them, mystical and magical, but in a way that's so real. In terms of Afro-Surrealism, there are a lot of conversations about what was happening in post-colonial society that made daily life quite surreal, but also there were quite serious conversations. I feel very attracted to it because of how a mystical landscape can be so relatable to reality somehow. The combination of rituals and traditional medicine in Nigeria (*Juju*) and the European culture of the idealism of travelling and going away — I like all those combinations of daily life. I am attracted to the fantastical and ritualistic aspect of Surrealism that grounds you in real life.

above Yasmina Atta, Kosmos in Blue, wings and bodysuit 01, 2020
left Yasmina Atta, Kosmos in Blue, wings, 2020

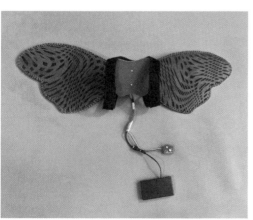

AS In your work, you draw inspiration from Senegalese film-makers such as Djibril Diop Mambéty, Mati Diop and Ousmane Sembène, who all delve into the surreal in their own ways. What drew you to their bodies of work?

above Model Donyale Luna in the film *Soft Self-Portrait of Salvador Dalí*, 1970
right Mr Brew, poster for *Sakobi: The Snake Girl*, 1998

YA With Nollywood, there wasn't enough discussion that I could find online, so I was attracted to the continuity of [Senegalese] film-makers. They have really strong female characters, who are going through completely different things, but I could then relate to the Surrealist influences in those movies and specifically to the women. A lot of the films have this concept of 'going abroad'. Mati Diop's *Atlantics* is quite dark and you see the reality of immigration. In Mambéty's *Touki Bouki*, the protagonists are really excited to go to France and they think this will solve all their problems. Throughout the movie, there's Josephine Baker's song 'Paris' playing. The surreal depiction of immigration, travelling and discovering, especially when you have so much where you are, it's quite interesting to me.

190

AS Where Afrofuturism deals with the future, science and the advancement of technology, Afro-Surrealism in contrast deals more with the present. Do you find yourself looking more at the future or focusing more on the now?

YA I think a lot about right now. I feel it's very grounding for me, especially with the internet and social media; you almost start to see things ten steps ahead, and because of this you are not really in the moment. Many of the older generation feel bad for us. Lately, I've been trying to be in the now and that's why I am interested in Afro-Surrealism rather than Afrofuturism, which doesn't feel as grounding. It feels almost escapist. [With Afro-Surrealism] it's quite hard to define because it doesn't really have an aesthetic to it, which I kind of love.

AS You mentioned mysticism as very important to you and essential for your design practice. Why do you think there's been a collective shift towards spiritualism in recent years?

Ousmane Sembène, *La Noire de ... (Black Girl)*, 1966

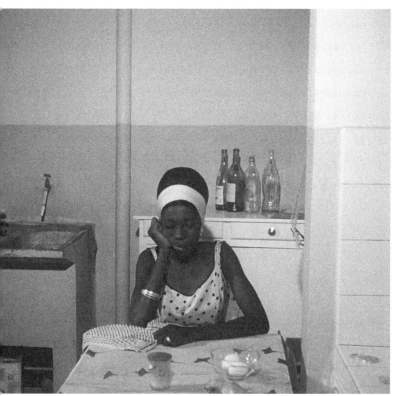

YA I think it's because of technology and the amount of data that we consume. I am reading this book at the moment called *The Disappearance of Rituals*, by Byung–Chul Han, and he talks about our lack of community and how we consume so much on the internet without anything grounding us. We consume so much data but nothing is retained, so I think a lot of people are looking for things that really stay with you. I keep saying that I like things that are grounding, but I think that we are returning to objects and stillness.

AS At the beginning of this interview, you were asked what three words come to mind when you think of Surrealism, and you said 'spirit', 'magic' and 'truth'. I feel we've talked about spirit and magic, so what truth do you look to impart to your work?

YA I try to have an honest approach. We've mentioned the playful aspect of my practice, and at a certain time I felt pressure to have a specific discourse behind what I was doing — forced to make something political, or that everything must mean something. I think it's important to be able to create without feeling the pressure to say something or to stand for something or have a political agenda. The truth comes from being genuine about making things and allowing people to interpret them how they'd like, rather than me imposing my idea of the work I am making. I'd rather the viewers make up their own minds and decide for themselves. Whether that's negative or positive, I don't mind. I am always really interested in knowing what people think, and I want to know their interpretation of my work — which sometimes is even more truthful than mine. ■■■■

Djibril Diop Mambéty, *Touki Bouki*, 1973

ARTIFICIAL

INTELLIGENCE

In the 1920s, the founding Surrealists created art and design with the everyday objects around them. Now those objects include technological tools and systems that shape our lives in ways beyond our individual understanding. We are only just beginning to feel the power of artificial intelligence (AI), itself a form of altered mind, to change our perception and experience of the world. As the field of AI art expands exponentially, AI is also impacting on contemporary design on both the functional and creative levels. Alongside scientists and engineers, artists and designers are engaged in calibrating AI's influence and potential.

Those at the forefront of AI research and development treat aesthetic considerations and art-making as crucial elements of their work. Alexander Mordvintsev, the researcher and engineer whose work led to the creation of Deep Dream in 2015, sees the creation of AI art as a form of applied research that allows him to experiment and innovate more freely. It is useful to think about parallels between the revolutionary impact of AI and that of the film camera in the 1930s. Will we soon become equally comfortable looking at the world through the eyes of intelligent machines?

64/1 (Karthik Kalyanaraman and Raghava KK) and Harshit Agrawal, *Strange Genders Manifestation 1 / 2, 2020*

Agrawal's work questions to what extent AI replicates human biases or presents us with unconventional new perspectives on reality. For this work, he trained two AI neural networks to recognise and draw stick figures of men and women. The training data consisted of hundreds of spontaneous stick drawings made by human volunteers for the project.

In the interview that follows, Blaise Agüera y Arcas characterises the operation of machine and human intelligence as a sequence of reactions and 're-mixes' that can never be written down or fully understood. Embracing AI means embracing the unknown, the unpredictable and the uncertain. Like so many new technologies in history, it has advocates and critics in equal measure. This unstable ground, it might be said, is Surrealism's special terrain.

Surrealism's legacy for contemporary design is both an aesthetic and an attitude. Above all, it is an effort to free the creative imagination from limits dictated by our conventional and current understanding of reality. The early Surrealists embraced the film camera. There is no doubt they would have been excited by AI and its ability to bring chance into the creative process in ways that human designers cannot fully predict or control. The 1924 *Manifesto of Surrealism* described a problem: 'experience is increasingly circumscribed. It paces back and forth in a cage from which it is more and more difficult to make it emerge'. Surrealism was born from a desire to unlock that cage. The question now is: Could AI be the key? ▪▪▪▪

This interview is between Justin McGuirk, chief curator at the Design Museum, and Blaise Agüera y Arcas, a VP fellow at Google. Previously a distinguished engineer at Microsoft, Agüera y Arcas is known for his work on artificial intelligence. His projects encompass augmented reality, machine learning, wearable technology and, most recently, a novella titled *Ubi Sunt*. From founding his own technology company in 2003 to establishing the Artists + Machine Intelligence programme at Google in 2016, Agüera y Arcas is a leading pioneer in the field of AI.

JUSTIN McGUIRRK & BLAISE AGÜERA Y ARCAS

JM Thinking about Surrealism's relevance today, I keep coming back to AI. We're cultivating new forms of intelligence, and using them to produce new dream-like imagery. But is this just metaphorical? The Surrealists were tapping into a pre-rational state, but AI is a highly rational product — it's computational. Are there parallels between Surrealist thought and AI image-making?

BAYA Absolutely. On a literal level, things like Dall-E 2 or Imagen make it simple to generate surreal images: you just ask and it happens. The fact that you use a language and what comes out is an image is interesting on a mechanical level and says something about the way language allows us to cook up combinations that

198

don't or can't exist in reality. By playing with language, we open up a space for the creation of impossible things, like mythologies.

We feel like we're tapping into 'the collective unconscious', or 'the archetypal' or something that has emerged from childhood trauma, which is Freud's version of all of this.

That's both true and illusory. It's true in the sense that language itself is cultural and it's a hyperobject that emerges over deep time. It's an illusion in that we may think we have some deep inner self but, actually, the Surrealist idea that you're opening a window on to a stable inner landscape is false. I think it's absolutely improvisational, and you're using grammar and construct.

JM Surrealism was partly a response to and reaction against mechanisation; it was a new way of expressing our humanity by opening that window on to the inner self, as you said. André Breton's pure psychic automatism enabled the artist to supress conscious control and let that inner being, or true self, out. We're not at the stage with AI and image-making of talking about consciousness. Does that matter?

BAYA I think the most important ingredient in Surrealism is representation, and I mean it in quite a nerdy way. I mean manifolds that allow for concepts and media — visual and auditory things, speech and ideas — to all be represented in relation to each other and in ways that can either be analysed or synthesised. That sounds kind of abstract, but it's literally what neural nets do nowadays. When you have an encoder and decoder of language and images and you ask it to do captioning or whatever, it's just working with that manifold.

JM So it's a representational tool?

BAYA Yes, it's representing the space of visual and textual concepts, and just playing in that representation. You start with a random number, you filter through it that representation and you get a Surrealist image. Or you start with some text and you get an image that you can style in different ways.

So it's a representation of something collective that is largely shared by all of us, even though we have our different languages and our different cultures.

JM You're saying that machine learning does represent a kind of collective unconscious, because it's being made by humans?

BAYA Yes. The idea that this is about the individual or the artist, that it's all very personal and subjective, is not really true. One sees that in a lot of Asian art. Who is the artist of the great terracotta army of Xian, or of the temples of Cambodia? These are hyperobjects. They don't have an artist. It's just humanity.

JM AI-generated images, like those of Deep Dream or Dall-E 2, are based on highly rational pattern recognition, but they have a dream-like status. Is this just a computational special effect? I'm talking about the visual manifestation, the rendering of these images so that two incongruous things can co-exist. How much is that innate to the machine learning? And how much is it a function of what it's trying to do, which is to morph two things together?

page 199 Google Deep Dream Zoom, *Mona Lisa redreamed*, 2022

BAYA I think it's both. In a way, it's a simple question: Are you taking two things and interpolating? And then finding the closest path between them on that manifold? Or are you feeding in random noise and then doing something? Eberhard Fetz, the neuroscientist at the University of Washington, likens Deep Dream to what happens during an acid trip.

JM But does Deep Dream look the way it does because of all the art produced after acid trips in the 1960s, or is it a coincidence?

BAYA I don't think it's a coincidence, but it's also not causal. The reason we know that is because Image Net, which was used to do all that old Deep Dream stuff in 2016, was not trained on any psychedelic hippy art. The images are all of common and natural objects. The fact that Deep Dream has that quality, I'm pretty sure is emergent. In other words, hippy art was a style of its time, but also a scientific observation about how vision works.

JM So there's a clear analogy between what happens when a computer tries to make these images and what happens when a brain on LSD is released to make these kinds of images?

BAYA This isn't a universally held view, but I believe so.

You've raised rationality a couple of times, and I want to interrogate that a bit. For me, there's nothing rational about neural nets. I also think that rationality is a bit of a chimera. As you probably know, Leibniz believed that we'd be able to rationalise everything. He imagined that we'd eventually come up with an algebra wherein one can write down any proposition — not just in maths, but also in politics, economics or religion. And the way he explained it was that two people can sit down with their slates, and then calculate who is right the same way you'd calculate a maths proof. That would be a triumph of rationality — to develop an algebra that could represent anything, and that could derive the rightness or wrongness of any position.

We still have Leibniz's idea of rationality in mind when we imagine cold and calculating robots, like Data from *Star Trek: The Next Generation*. That's actually what the good old-fashioned AI movement, which had all those winners and failures, was trying to do. It continued Leibniz's idea that if you write down enough facts and rules, you'd get something intelligent out of it. That's the way we imagine it should work, except that our thoughts are imperfect because of our irrationality, our emotions. That programme went nowhere. All those attempts to write down rules resulted in extraordinarily brittle systems.

So the scope of maths, the scope of rationality, is very limited.

Google Deep Dream Zoom, *A gateway between dreams*, 2022

JM And the Surrealist project of trying to distinguish the two, the rational and the unconscious or irrational, was also a false premise?

BAYA I think it was an entirely false premise; or it imagined that rationality could go further than it can. Even though the neural-nets approach is a computation, it's not a calculation. We often use the term algorithm now, and I kind of bristle at the term. An algorithm is a set of rational steps that you write down and that take you from A to B.

It's true that when you evaluate a neural net it does boil down to zillions of additions and multiplies. It's made of maths, in the same way that everything that goes on in our brains is made of maths, but it's not calculating a thing, and it's definitely not following an algorithm. If you write down the code, it's just a couple of screenfuls; it's the same no matter what the neural net has learned to do. It's just about calculating the inputs and sending the outputs to the next neuron — that's basically what the algorithm is, what the code is. It tells you nothing about what is actually going on. What's going on is all in the weights and in the activations, and is not subject to logic in any sense that we can write down and understand.

JM From what I've seen of Dall-E 2 — which is mainly people having fun with it on social media — it feels like a collage tool, a perfect Surrealist tool. Surrealists were interested in juxtapositions. It's also a wish-fulfilment tool – show me x meets y.

BAYA I don't see it as a collage tool. A collage literally means that you have a corpus of starting material and you take your scissors and you cut stuff out and then you paste it down.

JM You mean it's not searching Google for source material?

BAYA Not at all. Very large neural nets, like Imagen, are in the hundreds of billions of weights. They don't memorise the internet; they're not doing a search. It's a neural net that has figured out how to generalise concepts, visual ones or textual ones, and your prompts often generate random numbers that then are filtered through these representations, which then generate pixels or texts. It's by no means searching and fetching originals. In fact, the whole idea of learning, when we say machine learning, must imply generalisation. Generalisation means noticing the pattern and figuring out how to do it.

JM Finally, does AI help us expand the imagination and produce new forms of expression?

Alexander Mordvintsev, *deepdream.c*, 2015/2021

BAYA Yes. I'm not saying that AI art is poised to take over the job. My own view of invention and creation is that they're almost like chemical reactions that happen in people's brains. When certain ingredients are in the air, they recombine in people's brains to make certain outputs. There's no invention you can name that didn't have about eighteen simultaneous inventors, like the light bulb or the radio, for example. I see that with artistic styles as well. Why this synchronicity? Because people are immersed in a culture, and have certain ingredients already available to them. The brain reacts and these things get formed. That's why history has this exponential progression; there are more and more things in the environment to remix. So, of course, if AI can remix in the ways we've just been describing, then there are many more places in the world where that reaction can take place. ■

☰ BIOGRAPHIES

Glenn Adamson is a curator and writer who works at the intersection of craft, design history and contemporary art.

Susanna Brown is a curator, writer and lecturer specialising in photography and fashion.

Kathryn Johnson is the curator of *Objects of Desire: Surrealism and Design 1924 - Today* at the Design Museum, London.

Priya Khanchandani is Head of Curatorial and Interpretation at the Design Museum, London.

Alyce Mahon is Professor of Modern and Contemporary Art History at the University of Cambridge.

Tim Marlow is Chief Executive and Director of the Design Museum in London.

Justin McGuirk is Chief Curator at the Design Museum and Director of Future Observatory.

Ayoola Solarin is a TV writer, editor and arts journalist based in London.

Ghislaine Wood is the acting director of the Sainsbury Centre and research department fellow at the Victoria and Albert Museum.

ACKNOWLEDGEMENTS

This book was published to accompany the exhibition *Objects of Desire: Surrealism and Design 1924 - Today* at the Design Museum, London, 14 October 2022 to 19 February 2023. The exhibition was originally curated by the Vitra Design Museum in 2019.

Vitra Design Museum

Curator	Mateo Kries
Assistant Curator	Tanja Cunz
Exhibition Tour	Isabel Serbeto

The Design Museum

Curators	Kathryn Johnson
	Lucia Savi
Assistant Curator	Tiya Dahyabhai
Exhibition Project Manager	Gabria Lupone
Exhibition Coordinator	Georgia Mulvaney-Thomerson
Graphic Designer	Alexander Boxill Studio
Exhibition Designers	EMYL, Basel
	All Things Studio
	Alexander Boxill Studio
Layout Adaptation	René Herzogenrath

PICTURE CREDITS

Cover: Photo Markus Tollhopf. Courtesy Ingo Maurer GmbH.

64/1 (Karthik Kalyanaraman and Raghava KK) and Harshit Agrawal: p.196 **A** © ADAGP, Paris and DACS, London 2022: pp. 80-1, 108, 111l, 122, 126, 162, 168; akg-images/Denise Bellon. © ADAGP, Paris and DACS, London 2022: p.163; akg-images/Denise Bellon. © Orange County Citizens Foundation/ARS, NY and DACS, London 2022: p.164; Alain Sembène: p.193; Album/Alamy Stock Photo: p.31; Alexander Mordvintsev and the K21 Collection by Kanon: p.205; Almine Rech, © Allen Jones: p.159; Photo Andreas Sütterlin. © Vitra Design Museum: p.91; Andreas von Einsiedel/Alamy Stock Photo: pp.34-5; Photo Andy Keate. Courtesy of the artist and Friedman Benda: p.83; Photo Archivio Cameraphoto Epoche. Solomon R. Guggenheim Foundation. Gift, Cassa di Risparmio di Venezia, 2005: p.129; Archivo Lafuente: p.150; © ARS, NY and DACS, London 2022: p.169 **B** B&B Italia: p.50; BD Barcelona 1972 S.L.: p.30; Bettmann/GettyImages: p.130; © BLESS 2022: p.77; bpk/Nationalgalerie, SMB, Sammlung Scharf-Gerstenberg. © ADAGP, Paris and DACS, London 2022: p.165; Brooklyn Museum of Art, New York: p.70b **C** Photo Cappellini. © Kuramata Design Office: p.86; Photo Carlo Mollino. Courtesy Museo Casa Mollino, Turin: pp.42t, 43; Carpenters Workshop Gallery: pp.53, 89; Castle Studios and R & Company. Reproduced by permission of Castle Studios: p.66; Cecil Beaton/Condé Nast/Shutterstock: p.115; © Crown copyright. Historic England Archive: p.37; Photo Dallas Museum of Art. © ADAGP, Paris and DACS, London 2022: p.154 **D** Daniele Iodice: p.72; Photo Daniele Iodice. Courtesy Nilufar Gallery: pp. 84, 85; Created by Deep Dream Generator: pp.199, 203; Denise Bellon/akg-images. © Meret Oppenheim/DACS 2022: pp.170-1; © the Design Museum. Gift of the Conran Foundation: p.76; © Dior: p.133; Photo Dirk Rose. © Dunne & Raby: p.100; © Dunne & Raby: p.95 **E** © Edra: pp.55, 58; © Erik Madigan Heck. Courtesy Christophe Guye Galerie: p.106; © Estate of André Kertész. Courtesy of Stephen Bulger Gallery: p.167; © Estate of Art Smith: pp.70t, 71; Estudio Campana: pp.56, 57; Everett Collection Inc/Alamy Stock Photo: p. 114 **F** Photo Fernando Laszlo. Courtesy Estudio Campana: p.47; Friedman Benda and Jonathan Trayte: p.82; Front: p.93; Fundació Gala-Salvador Dalí, Figueres, 2022. Image Rights of Salvador Dalí reserved: pp.33, 128 **G** Gitta Gschwendtner: p.28; Gjon Mili/The LIFE Picture Collection/Shutterstock: p.92; Photo Hagen Sczech. Courtesy Ingo Maurer GmbH: p.79 **H** Photo Horst P. Horst. © Condé Nast: p.123 **I** Institut National de l'Audiovisuel (INA), France: p.190 **J** Photo Jason Evans: pp.97, 99; Jasper Morrison Studio: p.46; Photo Jean Tholance: p.160; Photo Jeon Byung-cheol. Courtesy of the artist. © Lee Bul: p.155; Jersey Heritage Trust, UK: pp. 124, 125; Photo John Hooper. Courtesy Friedman Benda and Jonathan Trayte: pp. 60-1 **K** Photo Karen Kalou: pp. 153, 173, 174, 175, 178, 179; Collection Kirkland Museum of Fine & Decorative Art, Denver: p.48 **L** Le Corbusier Foundation. © F.L.C./ADAGP, Paris and DACS, London 2022: p. 39; Le Corbusier Foundation: pp.40, 41; © Lee Miller Archives, England 2022. All rights reserved. leemiller.co.uk: p.127; © Estate of Leonora Carrington/ARS, NY and DACS, London 2022: p. 24; Photo Lorenzo Sampaolesi. © Archivio Nanda Vigo, Milano: p.51; Photo M. Lee Fatherree. Courtesy Marvin Lipofsky Studio, Inc.: p.64 **M** © Man Ray 2015 Trust/DACS, London 2022: p.146; © Man Ray 2015 Trust/DACS, London 2022: pp. 118b, 119, 120, 121; Photo Markus Tollhopf. Courtesy Ingo Maurer GmbH: p.78; Mary Katrantzou: p.132; Photo Mattia Tonelli. Courtesy Paradisoterrestre: p.52; © Moooi: p.49; Museo Casa Mollino, Turin: pp.32, 42b, 44, 45; The Museum of Modern Art, New York: p.183r **N** Najla el Zein: p.176; Najla El Zein and Friedman Benda: p.177; Photo Niels Fabæk. Courtesy of Nina Saunders: pp.20-1; Photo Nils Jorgensen/Alamy Live News. © ADAGP, Paris and DACS, London 2022: p.156 **P** Philadelphia Museum of Art, The Samuel S. White 3rd and Vera White Collection. © Man Ray 2015 Trust/DACS, London 2022: p.118t; Philadelphia Museum of Art. Gift of Mme Elsa Schiaparelli, 1969: p.105; Photo © Phillips Auctioneers Limited. © Kuramata Design Office: p.87; Photo Philippe Halsman © Philippe Halsman Estate 2022. Image Rights of Salvador Dalí reserved. Fundació Gala-Salvador Dalí, Figueres, 2022: p.131; Pim Top: p.73; Plaisir de France n°18, 1936: p.38 **R** Photo Red Saunders: pp.25, 27 **S** © Sarah Lucas. Courtesy of Sadie Coles HQ, London: p.145, 157; Schiaparelli: pp.116, 117, 149; Smithsonian American Art Museum. Museum purchase through the Smithsonian Institution Collections Acquisition Program. Reproduced by permission of Castle Studios: p.68; Studio Makkink & Bey: p.88; © Studio Bouroullec: pp.74, 75; © Succession Wolfgang Paalen: p.161 **T** Teemour Mambety: p.195; Telimage, Paris: p.166; © Tim Walker Studio: pp. 103, 109, 111r, 112-3; Toledo Museum of Art, Gift of Maurine B. Littleton and Carol Shay: p.63 **V** Vince Fraser: p.183l; © Vitra Design Museum. Photo Ludger Paffrath: pp. 13, 14, 19; © Viviane Sassen, courtesy Stevenson Gallery S-A: pp. 135, 139, 141, 143; Photo West Dean College of Arts and Conservation: p.36: Photo West Dean College of Arts and Conservation. © Salvador Dali, Fundació Gala-Salvador Dalí, DACS 2022: p.90; Courtesy XXO – Xtra Xtra Original. © ADAGP, Paris and DACS, London 2022: p.158 **Y** Yasmina Atta: pp.185, 187, 189 **Z** Zeb Ejiro Productions: p.191.

Design Museum Publishing
Design Museum Enterprises Ltd
224–238 Kensington High Street
London W8 6AG
United Kingdom

First published in 2022
© 2022 Design Museum Publishing

978-1-872005-62-1

Publishing Manager	Mark Cortes Favis
Editor	Kathryn Johnson
Picture Researcher	Anabel Navarro
Editorial Assistants	Stefano Mancin and Tiya Dahyabhai
Copyeditors	Simon Coppock and Denny Einav
Proofreader	Ian McDonald
Designer	Alexander Boxill Studio

Many colleagues at the Design Museum have supported
this book, and thanks go to them all.

Distribution	**UK, Europe and select territories around the world**
	Thames & Hudson
	181A High Holborn
	London WC1V 7QX
	United Kingdom
	thamesandhudson.com
	USA and Canada
	ARTBOOK	D.A.P.
	75 Broad Street, Suite 630
	New York, NY 10004
	United States of America
	www.artbook.com
Printed & Bound	J. Thomson, UK